D1739921

A BOOK OF
ENGLISH PROVERBS

Mr. Collins, having established a reputation by
his work on English usage in three books on
synonyms, and two on idioms, has now turned
to a new field. Proverbs have been strangely
neglected from the point of view of the reader
who wants something more than a dictionary
as a reference book, or than a mere list giving the
briefest of definitions. Mr. Collins's treatment
is a happy compromise between these two types
of book. He confines himself to proverbs that
are current, and to what, in contrast to merely
proverbial phrases, are maxims; and supplies in
his well-known pithy, light style, short explana-
tions.

For a reader whose interest in proverbs leads him
a little further than their present use Mr. Collins
adds an agreeable spice of scholarship by often
quoting early anticipations of a proverb, before
it became crystallized in its current form, found
for example in Chaucer, the Bible, Shakespeare,
the early collectors of proverbs, and sometimes
modern writers.

A BOOK OF
ENGLISH
PROVERBS

WITH ORIGINS AND EXPLANATIONS

by
V. H. COLLINS

GREENWOOD PRESS, PUBLISHERS
WESTPORT, CONNECTICUT

Library of Congress Cataloging in Publication Data

Collins, Vere Henry.
  A book of English proverbs.

    Reprint of the ed. published by Longman, London.
    Includes bibliographies.
    1. Proverbs, English. I. Title.
[PN6421.C6 1974]   398.9'21   73-16945
ISBN 0-8371-7242-X

© *V.H. Collins 1959*

All rights reserved
No part of this publication may be reproduced, stored in a retrieval
system, or transmitted in any form or by any means, electronic,
mechanical, photocopying, recording, or otherwise, without the
prior permission of the Copyright owner

First published in 1959 by Longman Group Ltd.

Reprinted with the permission of Longman Group Ltd.

Reprinted in 1974 by Greenwood Press,
a division of Williamhouse-Regency Inc.

Library of Congress Catalogue Card Number 73-16945

ISBN 0-8371-7242-X

Printed in the United States of America

CONTENTS

[v]

PREFACE

THIS book is a collection of the chief proverbial sayings that are current today. The term 'proverbial saying' is interpreted as implying a 'generalised statement', including injunctions, and not merely an idiomatic phrase, to cover which the word 'proverb' is sometimes loosely used. Thus such expressions as 'His fingers are all thumbs' or 'Raining cats and dogs' would not be considered as coming within the scope of the present collection. Subject to this restriction the term is allowed to cover statements though they are in a form in which there is an ellipsis. Thus 'Better late than never', 'Words not deeds', 'Like father, like son', are classed as such.

The term is used also to cover 'maxims'. (The words 'adage' and 'saw' are almost obsolete.) 'Proverb' and 'maxim', as commonly used, often overlap. Strictly 'maxim' generally applies to a rule for conduct; 'proverb' to what, universally, happens or is true.

In addition to proverbs and maxims some quotations from literature are given that can be regarded as having become integrated parts of the spoken and written language. There have been added moreover some other proverbs from foreign languages both ancient and modern that are in such common use in English speech and writing that their inclusion also has been thought not to invalidate the use in the the title of the word 'English'.

In tracing the origins of proverbial sayings their early introduction into our language in Early English or later is of great interest, and often of importance; but corresponding sayings in classical Greek and Latin are often given, whether or not they may be thought to be the origin of the present established and current proverb. Occasionally corresponding proverbs in modern foreign languages have also been given.

Proverbs have not been excluded on the truth of which there might be controversial opinions; nor those that are not universally, but only in some circumstances, true; nor even some that are manifest exaggerations; but there have usually been excluded those that seemed undoubtedly false, such as *There is no pleasure without pain, While there is life there is hope, It is the unforeseen (or unexpected) that always happens.* (There is, less common, a variation of the last of these, with *often* instead of *always*; but that, though less false, seemed too trite to deserve inclusion.)

Attention is drawn to a proverb when there exists another expressing an exactly opposite statement.

Some of those who have read my two books on idioms may notice that this book includes a few proverbs (about two dozen altogether) that have already been treated in those. The explanation is that, when the project of a book on proverbs first came into my mind, *A Book of English Idioms* was already published, and its sequel had been accepted for publication, and had reached a stage where deletions of articles would have meant not only serious dislocation, and extensive renumbering in the list of idioms, the articles, the index, and the cross-references, but also inconvenient delay. I ask readers' forgiveness for the repetition involved in the reappearance of those articles here.

The citations of early records and adumbrations, before a proverb became crystallised and established in its current form, have usually been based on the *Oxford Dictionary of English Proverbs.* For the many references to and quotations from that book I am again greatly indebted, as I have had occasion to be on previous occasions for other books on usage, to the Delegates of the Clarendon Press for the generous leave they have given.

Much supplementary information and help have been gained from that great, erudite, scholarly and important book, Mr. Burton Stevenson's *Proverbs, Maxims, and Familiar Phrases*.

In addition to these two books additional information has often been gained from G. L. Apperson's *English Proverbs and Proverbial Phrases* (1929).

Frequent citation of the following ·seven collections of proverbs has been made by mention of only the author, without on each occasion giving the title of the book:

R. Taverner, *Proverbs or Adages*, 1539;

J. Heywood, *A Dialogue containing the Proverbs in the English Language*, 1546;

T. Draxe, *Bibliotheca Scholastica*, 1616;

G. Herbert, *Outlandish Proverbs*, 1640;

T. Fuller, *The History of the Worthies of England*, 1662;

J. Ray, *A Collection of English Proverbs*, 1670;

J. Kelly, *A Complete Collection of Scottish Proverbs*, 1721;

T. Fuller, *Gnomologia*, 1732.

It is remarkable that we owe much of our knowledge of the history of proverbs to the energy and versatility of George Herbert, a poet and a divine, and of Heywood, a writer of plays and ballads. On the other hand the reference to Fuller is always to the physician (1654–1744), whose published work included *Gnomologia* mentioned above, unless his namesake, Thomas Fuller the divine (1608–61), is particularised.

For convenience in constant reference the *Oxford Dictionary of English Proverbs* (recently revised by Sir Paul Harvey) is cited as *O.D.E.P.* The following abbreviations have also been used:

R. for the record of the date of the earliest use of a proverbial saying in its current form.

A. for the record of the date of an adumbration of what later crystallised into and became established as a proverbial saying.

Both in the general scheme for the book and in much of its detailed execution I have been constantly, valuably, and deeply, indebted for advice and help to Mr. G. D. H. Pidcock.

LIST OF PROVERBS

1 Absence makes the heart grow fonder.
2 Accidents will happen in the best regulated families.
3 A wise man is never less alone than when he is alone.
4 A soft answer turneth away wrath.
5 Art is long, life is short.
6 Out of the mouths of babes and sucklings.
7 No man ever became thoroughly bad at once.
8 A thing of beauty is a joy for ever.
9 Beauty is but skin-deep.
10 As you make your bed, so you must lie on it.
11 A swarm of bees in May is worth a load of hay, but a swarm
   in July is not worth a fly.
12 Beggars cannot be (*or* must, *or* should be, no) choosers.
13 Everything must have a beginning.
14 Believe not all that you see nor half what you hear.
15 The best is often the enemy of the good.
16 The best is yet to be.
17 He is the best general who makes the fewest mistakes.
18 A bird in the hand is worth two in the bush.
19 Birds of a feather flock together.
20 *Bis dat qui cito dat.*
21 Two blacks do not make a white.
22 If the blind lead the blind, both will fall into a ditch.
23 None are so blind as those who will not see.
24 Blood is thicker than water.
25 The blood of the martyrs is the seed of the church.
26 One cannot get blood (*or* water) from a stone.
27 Of the making of books there is no end.
28 You cannot have it both ways.
29 Boys will be boys.
30 What is bred in the bone will not out of the flesh.
31 Brevity is the soul of wit.

32 A bully is always a coward.
33 A burnt child dreads the fire.
34 Busiest men find (*or* have) the most time (*or* leisure).
35 Everybody's business is nobody's business.
36 Let bygones be bygones.
37 Care killed the cat.
38 A cat has nine lives.
39 When the cat is away the mice play (*or* will, *or* may, play).
40 First catch your hare.
41 Old birds are not caught with chaff.
42 A chain is no stronger than its weakest link.
43 *Nous avons changé tout cela.*
44 *Plus ça change, plus ça reste la même chose.*
45 Charity begins at home.
46 *Cherchez la femme.*
47 The child is father of the man.
48 Christmas comes but once a year.
49 Circumstances alter cases.
50 Cleanliness is next to godliness.
51 Every cloud has a silver lining.
52 Cast ne'er a clout till May is out.
53 The cobbler should stick to his last.
54 Let 'em all come.
55 Coming events cast their shadows before.
56 Two is company, but three is none.
57 Comparisons are odious.
58 Constant dropping wears (*or* will wear) away a stone.
59 Too many cooks spoil the broth.
60 Do not count (*or* reckon) your chickens before they are
      hatched.
61 God made the country and man made the town.
62 Corruption of the best becomes the worst.
62a Cowards die often (*or* many times) before their death.
63 Many would be cowards if they durst.
64 A creaking gate (*or* door) hangs long on its hinges.
65 No cross, no crown.
66 Do not cross the bridge before you come (*or* get) to it.
67 It is no use crying over spilt milk.
68 What can't be cured must be endured.

69 Curses, like chickens, come home to roost.
70 The darkest hour is that before the dawn.
71 The darkest place is under the candlestick.
72 Better be an old man's darling than a young man's **slave**.
72a Murder your darlings.
73 The longest day has (*or* must have) an end.
74 Dead men tell no tales.
75 None (are) so deaf as those who will not hear.
76 Death is the grand leveller.
77 Many deaths have place in men before they come to die.
78 Short debts (*or* reckonings) make long friends.
79 Deeds, not words.
80 Every man has the defects of his qualities (*or* virtues).
81 The woman who deliberates (*or* hesitates) is lost.
82 Better the devil you know than the devil you don't.
83 He should have (*or* He needs) a long spoon who sups with the devil.
84 Desperate diseases need (*or* must have) desperate cures (*or* remedies).
85 Fling dirt enough and some will stick.
86 Discretion is the better part of valour.
87 There's a divinity that shapes our ends, rough-hew them how we will.
88 Do as you would be done by.
89 Do as I say, not as I do.
90 Dog does not eat dog.
91 Every dog has his day.
92 Give a dog a bad (*or* ill) name, and hang him.
93 It is dogged that does it.
94 Let sleeping dogs lie.
95 Dreams go by contraries.
96 A drowning man will clutch (*or* catch) at a straw.
97 Golden lads and girls all must, as chimney-sweepers, come to dust.
98 Early to bed and early to rise makes a man healthy, wealthy and wise.
99 The early bird catches the worm.
100 (a) Easy, (b) Light (*or* Lightly), (c) Quickly, come; easy, etc., go.

[3]

101 One cannot eat one's cake and have it.
102 *Eheu fugaces.*
103 The end crowns all (*or* the work).
104 Look to (*or* Mark) the end.
105 Better an open enemy than a false friend.
106 The way to an Englishman's heart is through his stomach.
107 Enough is as good as a feast.
108 To err is human.
109 Every man for himself, and the devil take the hindmost.
110 Every man is the architect of his own fortunes.
111 Evil communications corrupt good manners.
112 For every evil under the sun there is a remedy or there is
 none.
113 Of two evils choose the less (*or* the least).
114 Example is better than precept.
115 The exception proves the rule.
116 Exchange (*or* A fair exchange) is no robbery.
117 Blessed is he who expects nothing, for he will never be disappointed.
118 He who excuses himself accuses himself.
119 Extremes meet.
120 That is all my eye.
121 What the eye does not see the heart does not grieve.
122 Four eyes see more (*or* better) than two.
123 *Facilis descensus Averni.*
124 Fact (*or* Truth) is stranger than fiction.
125 Facts are stubborn things.
126 Faint heart never won fair lady.
127 All is fair in love and war.
128 The falling out of lovers is the renewing of love.
129 Familiarity breeds contempt.
130 The farthest (*or* longest) way round (*or* about) is the nearest (*or* shortest) way home.
131 Fast (*or* Safe, *or* Sure) bind, fast, etc., find.
132 Like father, like son.
133 *Fiat justitia, ruat coelum.*
134 He who fights and runs away may live to fight another day.
135 Fine feathers make fine birds.
136 First impressions are half the battle (*or* are most lasting).

[4]

137 There are as good fish in the sea as ever came out of it.
138 Big fleas have little fleas.
139 Many a flower is born to blush unseen.
140 A fool and his money are soon parted.
141 There is no fool like an old fool.
142 A fool's bolt is soon shot.
143 Forbidden fruit is sweet.
144 Forewarned (is) forearmed.
145 Fortune knocks once at least at every man's gate (*or* door).
146 A friend to all (*or* everybody) is a friend to none (*or* nobody).
147 A friend in need is a friend indeed.
148 God defend (*or* deliver, *or* preserve) me from my friends.
149 By their fruits ye shall know them.
150 Gather ye rosebuds while ye may.
151 Do not look a gift horse in the mouth.
152 It is more blessed to give than to receive.
153 Those who live in glass houses should not throw stones.
154 The paths of glory lead but to the grave.
155 God's mill grinds (*or* mills grind) slow but sure.
156 God's in his heaven; all's right with the world.
157 God (*or* Heaven) helps those who help themselves.
158 Whom the gods love die young.
159 All is not gold that glitters.
160 The good is the enemy of the best.
161 One good turn deserves (*or* asks, *or* requires) another.
162 There is nothing either good or bad but thinking makes it so.
163 Grasp all, lose all.
164 When Greek meets Greek, then comes the tug of war.
165 A green Christmas (*or* Yule, *or* winter) makes a full (*or* fat)
    churchyard.
166 Half a loaf is better than no bread.
167 Many hands make light (*or* quick, *or* slight) work.
168 Handsome is that (*or* as, *or* who) handsome does.
169 As good (*or* well) be hanged for a sheep as a lamb.
170 Happy is the country that has no history.
171 Call no man happy until he is dead (*or* dies).
172 (The) more haste, (the) less (*or* worse) speed.
173 Make haste slowly.
174 Make hay while the sun shines.

175 Two (*or* Many) heads are better than one.
176 Kind hearts are more than coronets.
177 It is a poor heart that never rejoices.
178 Hell has no fury like a woman scorned.
179 Hell is paved with good intentions.
180 No man is a hero to his valet.
181 History repeats itself.
182 Hitch your wagon to a star.
183 Home is home, though it be never so homely.
184 There is no place like home.
185 East or west, home is best.
186 Even Homer sometimes nods.
187 Honesty is the best policy.
188 *Honi soit qui mal y pense.*
189 Honour to whom honour is due.
190 There is honour among thieves.
191 Hope deferred makes (*or* maketh) the heart sick.
192 Hope springs eternal.
193 Without (*or* If it were not for) hope, the heart would break.
194 He who has a wife and children has given hostages to fortune.
195 One crowded hour of glorious life is worth an age without a name.
196 A man's (*or* an Englishman's) house is his castle.
197 Hunger is the best sauce.
198 Idle folks have the least leisure.
199 Where ignorance is bliss, 'tis folly to be wise.
200 There is no ill in life that is not worse without bread.
201 Ill weeds grow apace (*or* fast).
202 It is an ill wind that blows nobody good (*or* any good).
203 Ill-gotten goods never prosper.
204 In for a penny, in for a pound.
205 A Jack of all trades is master of none.
206 Every Jack has (*or* must have) his Jill.
207 Judge not, that ye be not judged.
208 Be just before you are generous.
209 The king can do no wrong.
210 Know thyself.
211 More know Tom Fool than Tom Fool knows.

[6]

212 You never know what you can do till you try.
213 Knowledge is power.
214 He knows how many (blue) beans make five.
215 The labourer is worthy of his hire.
216 Lancashire thinks today what all England will think tomorrow.
217 The last straw breaks the camel's back.
218 Better late than never.
219 It is too late to shut (*or* lock) the stable-door when the horse
is stolen.
219a Laugh and the world laughs with you; Weep and you weep
alone.
220 He laughs best who laughs last.
221 Hard cases make bad law.
222 A man may lead a horse to the water, but he cannot make it
drink.
223 A little learning is a dangerous thing.
224 Least said soonest (*or* is soonest) mended.
225 Leave (*or* Let) well alone.
226 Lend your money and lose your friend.
227 The leopard cannot change its spots.
228 Liberty is not licence.
229 There are lies, damned lies, and statistics.
230 Life is a pilgrimage.
231 Life is sweet.
232 Life is not all beer and skittles.
233 Like to like (*or* Like will to like).
234 One must draw the line somewhere.
235 Listeners hear no good of themselves.
236 Little drops of water, little grains of sand, Make the mighty
ocean and the pleasant land.
237 Little (*or* Small) pitchers have great (*or* long, *or* wide) ears.
238 Many a little makes a mickle.
239 We live and learn.
240 Live and let live.
241 A living dog is better than a dead lion.
242 It is a long lane that has no turning.
243 Look thy last on all things lovely every hour.
244 Look before you leap.

245 Lookers-on see most of the game.
246 Love is blind.
247 Love laughs at locksmiths.
248 Love little and love long.
249 Love is not love which alters when it alteration finds.
250 Love makes the world go round.
251 Love me, love my dog.
252 It is best to be off with the old love before one is on with the new.
253 The course of true love never did run smooth.
254 Greater love hath no man than this.
255 'Tis better to have loved and lost than never to have loved at all.
256 Lucky at cards, unlucky in love.
257 Every man is a fool or a physician at forty (*or* thirty).
258 The proper study of mankind is man.
259 Manners makyth (*or* make) man (*or* the man).
260 Many heads are better than one.
261 So many men (*or* heads) so many minds (*or* wits).
262 Marriage is a lottery.
263 Marriages are made in heaven.
264 A young man married is a young man marred.
265 Marry in haste, and repent at leisure.
266 Like master, like man.
267 A man cannot serve two masters.
268 *Maxima debetur puero reverentia.*
269 There is a mean (*or* measure) in all things.
270 One man's meat is another man's poison.
271 Every medal has its reverse.
272 *Memento mori.*
273 The quality of mercy is not strained.
274 *De minimis curat non lex.*
275 Misery (*or* Adversity) makes (*or* acquaints men with) strange bedfellows.
276 Misfortunes (*or* Troubles) seldom (*or* never) come singly (*or* alone).
277 The (*or* Our) worst misfortunes are those that never happen (*or* befall us).
278 He who makes no mistakes makes nothing.

279 A miss is as good as a mile.
280 Money begets (*or* breeds, *or* gets, *or* makes) money.
281 The love of money is the root of all evil.
282 Money is a good servant but a bad master.
283 Money is the sinews of war.
284 *De mortuis nil nisi bonum.*
285 If the mountain will not come to Mahomet, Mahomet must
    go to the mountain.
286 Murder will out.
287 Music has charms.
288 (1) What is, must be. (2) What has been, had to be.
289 What must be, must be.
290 Nature abhors a vacuum.
291 Nature will have its course.
292 One touch of nature makes the whole world kin.
293 Though you cast out nature with a fork, it will still return.
294 The nearer the bone, the sweeter the flesh.
295 Necessity is the mother of invention.
296 Necessity has (*or* knows) no law.
297 Needles and pins, needles and pins: When a man marries
    his trouble begins.
298 Needs must when the devil drives.
299 It is a foolish (*or* foul, *or* ill) bird that defiles (*or* fouls) its
    own nest.
300 He who handles a nettle tenderly is soonest stung.
301 Never do things by halves.
302 Never too late to mend.
303 Never is a long day.
304 Never too old (*or* late) to learn.
305 Never say die.
306 Never the time and the place and the loved one all together.
307 A new broom sweeps clean.
308 Ill news travels (*or* flies, *or* comes) fast (*or* apace).
309 There is nothing new under the sun.
310 No news is good news.
311 *Noblesse oblige.*
312 Nothing is so bad but it might have been worse.
313 Nothing comes from (*or* out of) nothing.
314 Nothing venture, nothing have.

315 The offender never pardons.
316 The old order changeth.
317 A man is as old as he feels, and a woman as old as she looks.
318 Omelets are not made without breaking (*or* breaking of) eggs.
319 One man may steal a horse while another may not look over the hedge.
320 One swallow does not make a summer.
321 He who pays the piper can call the tune.
322 If you want peace, be prepared for war.
323 Take care of the pence, and the pounds will take care of themselves.
324 A penny saved is a penny gained.
325 He who touches pitch will be defiled.
326 Pity is akin to love.
327 There is a place for everything, and everything in its place.
328 One cannot be in two places at once.
329 A poet is born, not made.
330 Politeness (*or* Civility) costs nothing.
331 Any port in a storm.
332 Poverty is no sin.
333 When poverty comes in at the door, love flies (*or* goes, *or* jumps, *or* leaps) out of (*or* at) the window.
334 Practice makes perfect.
335 Practise what you preach.
336 Put your trust in God, but keep your powder dry.
337 There is no time like the present.
338 Prevention is better than cure.
339 Every man has his price.
340 Pride will have (*or* comes before) a fall.
341 Procrastination is the thief of time.
342 The proof of the pudding is in the eating.
343 It is easy to prophesy after the event.
344 A prophet is not without honour save in his own country.
345 Man proposes (*or* and, *or* but), God disposes.
346 Providence is always on the side of the strongest battalions.
347 One cannot put back the clock.
348 Never put off till tomorrow what can be done (*or* you can do) today.

349 It takes two to make a quarrel.
350 *Quem* (or *Quos*) *Deus vult perdere prius dementat.*
351 Ask no questions and you will be told no lies.
352 The race is not to the swift, nor the battle to the strong.
353 Rain before seven, fine (*or* shine) before eleven.
354 It never (*or* seldom) rains but it pours.
355 Rats leave (*or* desert, *or* forsake) a sinking ship (*or* falling house).
356 Reading makes a full man, conference a ready man, writing an exact man.
357 Red sky in the morning is shepherd's (*or* sailor's) warning; red sky at night is the shepherd's (*or* sailor's) delight.
358 Always verify your references.
359 Render unto Caesar the things that are Caesar's and unto God the things that are God's.
360 Revenge is sweet.
361 A rolling stone gathers no moss.
362 Rome was not built in a day.
363 When you are at Rome do as the Romans do (*or* as Rome does).
364 There is no rose without a thorn.
365 There is no royal road to learning.
366 It is better to be safe than sorry.
367 It will be all the same (*or* one) a hundred (*or* thousand) years hence.
368 What is sauce for the goose is sauce for the gander.
369 Best laid schemes gang aft a-gley.
370 I see and approve the better course, but I follow the worse.
371 Seeing is believing.
372 Self-preservation is the first law of nature.
373 They also serve who only stand and wait.
374 A secret between more than two is no secret.
375 Catch not at the shadow and lose the substance.
376 Out of sight, out of mind.
377 Silence gives consent.
378 You cannot make a silk purse out of a sow's ear.
379 If you sing before breakfast, you'll cry before night (*or* dinner).
380 There is many a slip between the cup and the lip.

[11]

381 Slow and (*or* but) sure.
382 No smoke without fire.
383 I am the captain of my soul.
384 One sows and another reaps.
385 As you sow, so will you reap.
386 A spaniel, a woman, and a walnut tree, the more they're
    beaten the better they be.
387 Spare the rod and spoil the child.
388 Speech is silver, but silence is gold.
389 The spirit is willing, but the flesh is weak.
390 A staff (*or* stick) is quickly found to beat a dog with.
391 Still waters run deep.
392 A stitch in time saves nine.
393 Stolen waters (*or* pleasures) are sweet (*or* sweetest).
394 A straw may show which way the wind blows.
395 Strike while the iron is hot.
396 There is but one step from the sublime to the ridiculous.
397 Nothing succeeds like success.
398 Sufficient unto (*or* to) the day.
399 Let not the sun go down upon thy wrath.
400 Do not swap horses when crossing a stream.
401 Our sweetest songs are those that tell of saddest thought.
402 Take things as they come.
403 Talk of the devil, and he is sure to appear.
403a Never spoil a ship for a haporth of tar.
404 Every man (*or* one) to his (*or* one's) taste (*or* own taste).
405 There is no accounting for tastes.
405a Give a thief enough rope and he will hang himself.
406 Second thoughts are best.
407 Threatened folk (*or* folks, *or* men) live long.
408 A tide taken at the flood leads on to fortune.
409 Time flies.
410 Time is the great healer.
411 Time marches on.
412 Time is money.
413 There is a time to speak and a time to be silent.
414 Time and tide wait (*or* stay, *or* tarry) for no man.
415 Take time by the forelock.
416 *Timeo Danaos et dona ferentes.*

[12]

417 Times change.
418 A bad (*or* ill) workman quarrels with (*or* blames) his tools.
419 Every man to his trade (*or* craft, *or* business).
419a It is better to travel hopefully than to arrive.
420 Never trouble trouble till trouble troubles you.
421 Don't meet troubles half way.
422 Many a true word is spoken in jest.
423 Truth lies at the bottom of a well.
423a Truth is stranger than fiction.
424 Truth will prevail.
425 Union is strength.
426 *Verb. sap.*
427 *In vino veritas.*
428 Virtue is its own reward.
429 The voice of the people is the voice of God.
430 Everything comes to him who waits.
431 Walls have ears.
432 It is magnificent, but it is not war.
433 One should not wash one's dirty linen in public.
434 Waste not, want not.
435 A watched pot never boils.
436 Wilful waste makes woeful want.
437 The weakest goes to the wall.
438 It is better to wear out than to rust out.
438a Even the weariest river winds somewhere safe to sea.
439 All is well that ends well.
440 Every why has a (*or* hath its) wherefore.
441 Where there's a will there's a way.
442 He who will not when he may, when he will (*or* would) he
    shall have nay.
443 God tempers the wind to the shorn lamb.
444 March winds and April showers bring forth May flowers.
445 Good wine needs no bush.
446 It is easy to be wise after the event.
447 Don't whistle (*or* halloo, *or* shout) until you are out of the
    wood.
448 The wish is father to the thought.
449 Fair (*or* fine) words butter no parsnips.
450 Hard words break no bones.

[13]

451 A woman's work is never done (*or* at an end).

451a Wonders will never cease.

452 Wonders last but nine days.

453 Work while it is day.

453a All work and no play makes Jack a dull boy.

454 Half (*or* One half of) the world knows not how the other half lives.

455 (a) As well (*or* good) be, (b) Better be, out of the world, (a) as, (b) than, out of the fashion.

456 It takes all sorts to make a world.

457 Even a worm will turn.

458 Two wrongs do not make a right.

459 Young men see visions; old men dream dreams.

460 If you want a thing well done, do it yourself.

PROVERBS

1

Absence makes the heart grow fonder. A. 1732, Fuller, *Gnomologia*, Absence sharpens love, presence strengthens it. **R.** 1850, Bayly, *Isle of Beauty*. Compare **Out of sight, out of mind** (376).

2

Accidents will happen in the best regulated families. R. 1823, Scott in *Peveril of the Peak* (who, however, has 'befall'). 1850, Dickens (who has 'occur'): 'My dear friend Copperfield', said Mr. Micawber, 'accidents in the best regulated families will occur'. 'Families' is sometimes used in a loose, general, sense, with reference to organisations, institutions, etc.

3

A wise man is never less alone than when alone. *A wise person when alone has all the occupation and interest he needs, for reflection and communing with himself.* The originator of this saying, in Latin, was Scipio Africanus the Elder. It was recorded, in some work now lost, by his contemporary, the Elder Cato, from whom it is quoted twice by Cicero (*De Officiis*, iii, i; *De Republica*, i, 27). In English literature its first mention is by Robert Greene, 1584.

4

A soft answer turneth away wrath. This is from the Bible, *Proverbs* 15, 1, in the Authorised Version (1611). Over two centuries earlier Wyclif's translation of the Hebrew is 'A soft answere breikith ire'.

5

Art is long, life is short. (This is sometimes stated in the reverse order, **Life is short, art is long.**) *The life of a man lasts only a short time, but art with its manifestations goes on for ever.* The dictum appears first in the Greek of Hippocrates (fifth century B.C.). The word that in the English proverb has been translated as 'art' is in the Greek *technē*, meaning there the 'study of medicine' ('to master which', Hippocrates said, 'a lifetime was not long enough'). In the Latin maxim, of which the first record is in Seneca (first century A.D.), and which is usually quoted *Vita brevis, ars longa,* the Greek word *techne* becomes *ars.*

Chaucer, The lyf so short, the craft so long to lerne. **R** 1630 (Brathwàit).

6

Out of the mouths of babes and sucklings. Figuratively the expression is used so (without a verb), not with reference to the young, but to mean that *wisdom often comes from the uneducated and ignorant.* It is an ellipsis of Christ's words, in *Matthew* 21, 16, Out of the mouth of babes and sucklings thou hast perfected praise. 'babes' is often misquoted 'fools'.

7

No man ever became thoroughly bad at once. *There must always be stages in which a person gradually goes from bad to worse.* The origin of this statement is almost certainly Juvenal's words *Nemo repente turpissimus fuit* (No-one has suddenly become very bad). In English literature Sir Philip Sidney in *Arcadia* (1590) applies the idea also to goodness as well as to evil: There is no man sodainely excellentlie good, or extremely evill.

8

A thing of beauty is a joy for ever. This is the first line of Keats's *Endymion* (1818).

9

Beauty is but skin-deep. Davies (of Hereford), 1616: Beauty's but skin-deepe.

10

As you make your bed, so you must lie on it. Figuratively, *one must suffer from, or endure the ill results of one's actions.* 1640, Herbert: He that makes his bed ill lies there. *O.D.E.P.* does not cite the proverb word for word in its current form.

11

A swarm of bees in May is worth a load of hay, but a swarm in July is not worth a fly. A. 1655, where the swarm in May is worth 'a cow and a bottle of hay'. (A meaning of 'bottle' is 'bundle'.) R 1773. 1878, Richard Jefferies adds: 'a swarm in June is worth a silver spoon'.

12

Beggars cannot be (*or* must, *or* should be, no) choosers. Figuratively, *if one is in a weak and dependent situation, one can't lay down conditions or be exacting in demands or terms.* 1546, Heywood: Folke saie alwaie, beggars should be no choosers.

[17]

13

Everything must have a beginning. A. Chaucer's *Troylus and Cryseyde*: For every thing a ginning hath it nede. 1566, Gascoigne: Everything hath a beginning.

14

Believe not all that you see nor half what you hear. A 1205, Yif thu ileust arhcne mon, Selde thu saelt wel don [If thou believest every man, seldom shalt thou do well]. *O.D.E.P.* does not give any date for the use of the current form, but it cites in 1853: Believe only half of what you see, and nothing that you hear.

15

The best is often the enemy of the good. *In aiming at an ideal that one fails to reach one often misses what, though short of the best, one should or would have been glad to gain.* The proverb is adumbrated by Shakespeare in *King Lear* I, iv): 'Striving to better, often we mar what's well'. The first record of it in its current form is not until two and a half centuries later, as a translation from the French, *Le mieux est l'ennemi du bien*.

There is, however, a modern proverb, though less known, that **The good is often the enemy of the best,** which insists that we should not be content with a second-best.

16

The best is yet to be. This is usually quoted, from Browning's *Rabbi Ben Ezra* (1864), in the sense in which it is there used, with reference to one's growing old: 'in the last of life, for which the first was made'.

17

He is the best general who makes the fewest mistakes. *All people make mistakes, and the cleverest is the one who makes only a few.* **R.** Sir Ian Hamilton (1907), quoting Napoleon, as 'the highest authority'.

18

A bird in the hand is worth two in the bush. *It is better to be in possession of one, even if it is only a small, thing than to have hopes or expectations based on something that is of greater value but is remote and doubtful.* 1470: Betyr ys a byrd in the hond than tweye in the wode. Later versions often vary in their estimate of the number of hoped-for birds that the one in your hand is worth. A *Commonplace Book* of 1530 says three; Heywood (1546), ten; and Ray (1678) is not satisfied with less than a hundred. In Lodge (1590) the birds become personified: Better possess the love of Aliena than catch frivolously at the shadow of Rosalynde. In 1620, by Skelton, 'wood' becomes 'bush', and the proverb is crystallised into its current form.

19

Birds of a feather flock together. *People of similar characters and tastes associate with one another.* In Latin the statement is cited in Cicero's *De Senectute* as 'an old proverb'. 1578, Byrds of a fether best flye together. **R.** 1828.

20

Bis dat qui cito dat (Latin). *He gives twice who gives quickly:* i.e. *promptness in giving increases the value of a gift and one's gratitude to the giver.* There was a Greek epigram beginning 'Quick favours are sweeter'. In Latin a collection of sayings of Publilius Syrus (who flourished about 45 B.C.) has: He gives a kindness to a needy man twice who gives it quickly. Publilius was so fond of the sentiment that in his work it appears in another slightly different form. The French have *Qui donne vite donne deux fois*; the Germans *Wer bald gibt, der doppelt gibt.*

Chaucer adumbrates the English proverb in

> For whoes yeveth a gift, or doth a grace,
> Do it by tyme, his thank is well the more.

There are variants by W. Wilson (1550), Skelton (1620), Ray (1670). The current English form is recorded first as used by Johnson (in Boswell's *Life*).

21

Two blacks do not make a white. 'blacks' = 'bad acts', 'sins'; 'a white' = 'a good act, a virtue'. *The repetition of an evil act, by the same, or its commission by another, person, does not make it a good one.* R 1721, Kelly.

22

If the blind lead the blind, both shall fall into the ditch. Figuratively, *If the ignorant are led by the ignorant, both will come to disaster.* The proverb is from *Matthew*, 15, 14.

23

None are so blind as those who will not see. The statement is generally used figuratively. Often 'are' is omitted before 'so'. *There are no people so difficult to convince or persuade as those who, being anxious not to change their minds, are obstinately determined not to listen to or read arguments that are against their beliefs.* Heywood, 1546, has: Who is so deafe, or so blinde as is hee, That wilfully will nother here nor see? In 1662 Fuller gives the proverb in its current form except for 'the' instead of the later and current 'those'. E. Fitzgerald, 1852, has the current form except for 'that' instead of 'who'.

Compare **None (are) so deaf as those who will not hear** (75).

Blood is thicker than water. *The bond created by blood-relationship is stronger than that created by other circumstances: marriage, friendship, business relations, etc.* There is an anecdote, purporting to explain the expression, of an American naval officer who, in 1859, finding the English in difficulties with the Chinese, went to their help, and in his dispatch to his government justified his interference by using these words. But over four centuries earlier, in 1422, Lydgate adumbrates the idea of the proverb:

> For naturelly blod will ay of kynde [always naturally]
> Draw vn-to blod, wher he may it fynde.

R. 1670, Ray.

The blood of the martyrs is the seed of the church. A. Tertullian (Latin), 'Semen est sanguis Christianorum' ['The blood of Christians is seed']. **R.** 1619 (but with 'was' instead of 'is').

One cannot get blood (*or* water) from a stone. *One cannot get sympathy etc. from a hard- or cold-hearted person.* As far back as 1580 Lyly has a reference to 'wringing water from a stone', and Robert Greene in 1592 to 'getting water out of a flint'. **R.** 1850, Dickens, *David Copperfield.*

27

Of the making of books there is no end. This is adapted from *Ecclesiastes* 12, 12: Of making many books there is no end. This reflection, many centuries before the invention of printing, continues 'and much study is a weariness of the flesh'.

28

You cannot have it both ways. *It is impossible to gain, benefit from, enjoy, two circumstances or conditions that are inconsistent with, incompatible with, opposed to, each other.*

I have not been able to find at what date the expression came into use.

Compare **One cannot eat one's cake and have it** (101).

29

Boys will be boys. A. 1681: Children will do like children. R. 1853, Thackeray.

30

What is bred in the bone will not out of the flesh. *What is inherited will not fail to show itself, and cannot be expelled.* A. 1481, Caxton: That whiche cleuid [What was cleaved to] by the bone myght not out of the flesshe. 1546, Heywood: It will not out of the fleshe that is bred in the bone. Variants are, by Florio, translating Montaigne, 1603, 'never', for 'not'; Defoe, 1719, 'go out', for 'out'.

Compare **Though you cast out nature with a fork, it will still return** (293).

31

Brevity is the soul of wit. R. *Hamlet* II, ii, 90.

[22]

A bully is always a coward. 1856 (Maria Edgeworth's *Ormond*): Mrs. M'Crule, who like all other bullies was a coward, lowered her voice. The truth of the proverb is doubtful and is treated by Lamb in his essays on 'Popular Fallacies', but the discussion is complicated by him in a disquisition on the difference between valour and brutality.

33

A burnt child dreads the fire. Figuratively, *when one has been injured by something one will be on one's guard against a similar experience.* 1300, Brend [burned] child fur dredeth. **R.** 1580, Lyly.

34

Busiest men find (*or* have) the most time (*or* leisure). A. 1854, Payn: It is my experience that the men who are really busiest have the most leisure for everything. On the other hand there is also a proverb **Idle folks have the least leisure.**

35

Everybody's business is nobody's business. *The work and duties that a person assumes everybody except himself will attend to is attended to by nobody, and remains neglected.* R. Cotgrave, 1611, Every bodies work is no bodies work. **R.** 1653, in Walton's *Compleat Angler*.

36

Let bygones be bygones. A. Homer, *Iliad*, XVIII, 12, (translated): But we will allow these things to have happened in the past, grieved though we may be. Heywood, 1546:

Let all things past pass. 1648, Nethersole, *Parables*: Let bygans be bygans. **R.** 1815.

37

Care killed the cat. This statement is usually uttered as a warning that to worry may undermine health, reduce a person to misery, and perhaps cause death.

One of the *Shirburn Ballads* (1585–1616) has

> Let care kill a catte,
> Wee'le laugh and be fatte.

Shakespeare has (*Much Ado About Nothing*, V, i) What though care killed a cat, thou hast mettle enough in thee to kill care.

Possibly there was a fable, of which no trace is now to be found, of a cat that was killed by care. On the other hand a cat is often taken as an example of an animal that is exceptionally immune from injuries. It may be held, however, that there is no inconsistency between the fabled nine lives of a cat and its being killed by care, the point being that even so tough a creature as this can fall a victim to it.

Probably the alliteration of three k sounds has contributed to the popularity of the proverb.

38

A cat has nine lives. A. 1525, Beaumont and Fletcher: as many lives as a cat. 1546, Heywood: A woman hath nyne lyues like a cat.

39

When the cat is away the mice play (*or* **will,** *or* **may, play**). *When the master or chief or superior is absent, the subordinates can stop work and do what they like.* **R.** 1607.

First catch your hare. Literally it is a truism that you cannot cook a hare until you have got it. The expression is used figuratively as an injunction or warning with reference to a particular project that there are difficulties to surmount before it can be carried out. The earliest date recorded for this figurative use of the expression is 1855, by Thackeray. (*catch* seems to be a translation of one meaning of the French *prendre* = to take, to catch.)

41

Old birds are not caught with chaff. Figuratively, *people of experience are not easily taken in.* **A.** 1481, Caxton: I am no byrde to be locked ne take [enclosed or taken] by chaf. I know wel ynowh good corn. **R.** 1668, Shadwell, *Sullen Lovers*: There's no catching old birds with chaff.

42

A chain is no stronger than its weakest link. Figuratively, *the net effectiveness of an arrangement is conditioned by the weakest part of it.* Thus in an argument the weakness of even one point may be fatal to the strength of the whole. **A.** 1887, Conan Doyle: No chain is stronger than its weakest link.

43

Nous avons changé toute cela (French). *We have changed all that.* From Molière's play *Le Médecin malgré lui* (II, vii). This was published in 1666, but Mr. Eric Partridge in his *Dictionary of Clichés* says that the sentence did not become established as an anglicism until the nineteenth century.

[25]

44

Plus ça change, plus ça reste la même chose. *The more it changes, the more it remains the same thing.* From a book called *Les Guêpes*, 1849, by Alphonse Karr, best known for another book, *Voyage autour de mon Jardin*.

45

Charity begins at home. This expression is commonly used today to mean that *one's family and other relatives have claims on one's generosity and liberality that should be satisfied before one extends them elsewhere.* R. 1641, R. Brome (dramatist). In 1380 Wyclif has: Charite schuld bigyne at hem-selfe. But, although the word 'charity' was used in Early English, with the meaning that it has now virtually monopolised, of benevolence, especially alms-giving to the poor, its most common meaning was 'love', 'affection'; often 'Christian love', as in the Bible in *I Corinthians* 13, in the passage ending 'but the greatest of these is charity'.

46

Cherchez la femme. Literally this is an imperative, 'Search for the woman', used with reference to the source of a trouble, mischief, complication. It is often used in a general sense, that there is a woman who is the source of the trouble. The phrase comes from a play by Dumas *père* in 1865 (*Les Mohicans de Paris*), where it is used in connection with crime; but the sentiment, of woman as the origin of trouble, is as old as Virgil (*Aeneid*, I, 364: *Dux femina facti*).

47

The child is father of the man. *Childhood shows the characteristics that will develop in the grown-up person.* The words come from Wordsworth's poem

My heart leaps up when I behold
A rainbow in the sky.
So was it when my life began,
So is it now I am a man;
So be it when I shall grow old.

The poem ends:

And I could wish my days to be
Bound each to each with natural piety.

Here the poet carries on the idea of fatherhood. Every present day is the child of yesterday, and should show filial piety towards it.

Perhaps Wordsworth took the general thought from Milton's *Paradise Regained*, IV, 220:

The childhood shows the man,
As morning shows the day.

48

Christmas comes but once a year. 1573. Tusser, *Five Hundreth Pointes of Good Husbandrie*: At Christmas play and make good cheere, for Christmas comes but once a yeere.

49

Circumstances alter cases. *What may apply in a general way, or sometimes, or usually, does not apply always, when conditions are different.* **A.** 1600: The circumstances doth make it good or ill. **R.** 1870, in Dickens's *Edwin Drood*.

50

Cleanliness is next to godliness. Bacon, 1605: Cleanness of body was ever deemed to proceed from a due reverence to God. **R.** 1791, Wesley, in a printed sermon, where inverted commas suggest he was quoting it as a proverb: Cleanliness is indeed next to godliness.

51

Every cloud has a silver lining. *In every trouble and difficulty there is hope or expectation of an improvement in the circumstances.* **A.** Milton's *Comus*

> Was I deceived, or did a sable cloud
> Turn forth her silver lining on the night?

R. 1885, Gilbert, *The Mikado*: There's a silver lining to every cloud.

52

Cast ne'er a clout till May is out. *Do not give up wearing your winter clothes until June.* The primary meaning of the Old English word 'clout' was a piece of cloth, leather, metal, etc. It is now obsolete except in this proverb, and meaning (1) a heavy blow with the hand, (2) a rough piece of household cloth. Opinions differ about the meaning 'till May is out'. Is the reference to (1) the beginning, or (2) the end, of the month; or (3) to the blossoming of the Mayflower? And if it is to (3), the difference in latitude, e.g. between Land's End and John o' Groats, may be accounted for, since the farther north, the colder, and the later the blossoming.

53

The cobbler should stick to his last. *People should not meddle in matters outside their knowledge and experience.* The selection of a cobbler as typical of a person who should stick to his business is found in the elder Pliny's *Natural History*. In English the proverb is given by Taverner in 1539 as: Let not the shoemaker go beyond hys shoe; and by Lyly in 1579: The shoemaker must not go beyond his latchet, nor the hedger meddle with anything but his bill. **R.** Kelly, 1721.

[28]

54

Let them all come. A colloquial ejaculation of defiance to possible or threatening enemies. Compare *King John*, last lines: Come the three corners of the world in arms.

55

Coming events cast their shadows before. *Early signs foretell what is going to happen.* **R.** 1803. This proverb is generally applied to events that are undesirable.

56

Two is company, but three is none. *O.D.E.P.* quotes *Notes and Queries* as stating in 1871 that this was a common Lancashire proverb.

57

Comparisons are odious. *c.* 1440, Lydgate: Odyous of olde been comparisonis. Often found from the fifteenth century onwards.

Dogberry's malapropism, 'Comparisons are odorous' (*Much Ado*, III, v.) is anticipated about 1570 by an old comedy *Sir Gyles Goosecap*, Coparisons . . . be odorous, which also perhaps suggested the 'Caparisons don't become a young woman' of Mrs. Malaprop in Sheridan's *The Rivals* (1775).

58

Constant dropping wears (*or* will wear) away a stone. This metaphor is found in a Greek writer, Choerilus, in the fifth century B.C. An unknown Latin writer (*c.* 1050, partly quoting Ovid, A.D. 18) has *Gutta cavat lapidem non vi sed saepe cadendo* [A drop of water makes a hole in a stone not by violence but by frequent falling]. 1200, *Ancren*

Riwle: Luttle dropen thurleth thene vlint that ofte falleth thereon [Little drops pierce the flint that often fall upon it]. *Job*, 14, 19, The waters wear the stones **R**. 1874

The proverb is now generally used figuratively for the effects produced by action in a small matter, persisted in for a long time, e.g. to the influence of repetition by talking, in wearing down a person's will.

59

Too many cooks spoil the broth. *The work done in a job, enterprise, project, is spoilt if too many people are employed in it.* **A.** 1575, The more cooks the worse potage. **R**. 1662. Contrast **Many hands make light work** (167).

60

Do not count (*or* reckon) your chickens before they are hatched. *Do not assume you will have a thing, or do not make plans about it, before the conditions are realised, or the event has happened, etc.* Æsop has a fable with this moral. 1575, Howell: Count not thy Chickens that unhatched be. **R**. 1670, Ray.

61

God made the country and man made the town. The Latin writer Varro (116–27 B.C.) has *Nec mirum, quod divina natura dedit agros, ars humana edificavit urbes* [Nor is it wonderful, because divine nature gave us the fields, but the art of man built cities]. **R**. 1783, Cowper, *The Task*.

62

Corruption of the best becomes the worst. This is a translation of a Latin dictum, *Corruptio optimi pessima*, found in St. Thomas Aquinas *c.* 1270. **A.** Shakespeare's *Sonnets*, 94: For sweetest things turn sourest by their deeds; Lilies

[30]

that fester smell far worse than weeds. 1618, Bishop Joseph Hall: But there is nothing so ill as the corruption of the best.

62a

Cowards die often. *Cowards are so obsessed by fear of dying, from which brave people are free, that before they die they have many times suffered the experience of death.* This is said by Julius Caesar (II. i. 32), 'Cowards die many times before their deaths'. Three years earlier Drayton (1596) wrote 'Every houre he dyes, which ever feares'.

63

Many would be cowards if they durst. 1695, W. Morgan.

64

A creaking gate (*or* door) hangs long on its hinges. This expression is generally used figuratively of an invalid who lives much longer than was expected. 1776, T. Cogan, *John Bunch, Junior*: But they say a creaking gate goes the longest upon its hinges. R. 1913.
Compare **Threatened folk live long** (407).

65

No cross, no crown. *It is only by endurance, effort, suffering, that glory or beatitude is to be attained.* Quarles, 1621, The way to Blisse lyes not on beds of Downe, And he that had no Crosse deserues no Crowne. The metaphor is used in the title of a book by William Penn, in 1669, *No Cross, No Crown*: a Discourse showing that the daily bearing of Christ's Cross is the only way to the rest and kingdom of God.

66

Do not cross the bridge before you come (*or* get) to it.
Figuratively, *Do not take steps to deal with a difficulty,
trouble, problem, until it occurs, and immediate action becomes necessary.* Literally the injunction is absurd: how
could you cross a bridge before you came to it? The meaning is that you should not in your mind prematurely concern
yourself with a matter. *O.D.E.P.* gives 1895 as the date of
its earliest record in print. Mr. A. Johnson in *Common
English Proverbs* points out that in old days bridges were
often so badly built and dangerous that crossing them
needed care and courage, and caused travellers anxiety.
Compare **Do not meet troubles halfway (421).**

67

It is no use crying over spilt milk. *It is useless to indulge
in regrets for what has been done and cannot be remedied.*
The first record given by *O.D.E.P.*, in 1484, is of a figurative
adumbration: Take no sorrowe of the thynge lost whiche
may not be recouered. 1659, No weeping for shed milk.
1738, Swift: 'Tis a folly to cry for spilt milk. **R.** 1884. J.
Payn, *The Canon's Ward*: There's no use in crying over spilt
milk.

68

What can't be cured must be endured. A. 1377, Langland:
For qant *oportet* vyent en place yl ny ad que *pati* [For when
must comes forward, there is nothing for it but to *suffer*].
R. 1693, Motteux's translation of Rabelais.

69

Curses, like chickens, come home to roost. *Curses recoil
on the utterer.* **A.** (1) 1275, *Proverbs of Alfred*: Eueryches
monnes dom to his owere dure churreth [Every man's

judgment rebounds on to himself]. (2) Chaucer: And ofte tyme swich cursynge wrongfully retorneth agayn to hym that curseth, as a bryd that retorneth agayn to hys owene nest. R. 1810, Southey, *Curse of Kehama*. Today the proverb is generally used with reference, not to direct cursing, but to wishing or hoping that ill may befall a person or scheme, etc.

70

The darkest hour is that before the dawn. Figuratively, *things are often at their worst just before they get better; or the worst stage is often the prelude to an improvement.* 1650, Fuller. 1849, Charlotte Brontë, *Shirley*: This is a terrible hour, but it is often the darkest point which precedes the rise of day.

Compare the statement 'Things will have to get worse before they get better'.

71

The darkest place is under the candlestick. *A chief person in a firm, organisation, etc., whom one might expect to be more familiar with all the inmost secrets than anybody else, is often surprisingly ignorant of what is common knowledge.* I have been unable to find when this proverb was first used, but it is quoted as a proverb in 1902 in Belasco's play *The Darling of the Gods*.

72

Better be an old man's darling than a young man's slave. Heywood, 1546. In early versions there are variants, from 'slave', of 'worldling'; 'warling', which *O.D.E.P.* defines as 'one who is despised or disliked'; and, Scottish, 'wonderling'.

[33]

72a

Murder your darlings. *Be ready ruthlessly to stop using, or, if used, to delete from your manuscript or proofs, words, phrases, and images, that in the past have been great favourites of yours, but that on reconsideration you decide you, or others, are inclined to overwork, and thus are not fresh and vigorous.*

73

The longest day has (*or* must have) an end. The expression is generally used figuratively and with reference to a troublesome, painful experience. **A.** 1390, Gower, *Confessio Amantis*: Bot hou so that the dai be long, The derke nyht comth ate laste. Hawes, *c.* 1509: For though the day be never so longe, At last the belles ringth to evensonge. 1614, W. Camden: The longest day hath his end. 1659, Howell: The longest day hath an end.

74

Dead men tell no tales. The implication is that, if a man witnesses a crime, he should be killed so as to be unable to testify against the criminal. 'Dead' here means 'Murdered' 1663, The dead can tell no tales. **R.** Dryden, 1681.

75

None (are) so deaf as those who will not hear. The statement is generally used figuratively. *There are no people so difficult to make pay attention as those who are obstinately determined not to listen to arguments that are against their beliefs, wishes, etc.* 1546, Heywood: Who is so deafe or so blynde as is hee That wilfully will nother here nor see?

Compare **None are so blind as those who will not see** (23).

Death is the grand leveller, i.e., as making all men equal, the famous and the insignificant; rich and poor; wise and foolish; good and bad; happy and miserable. **A.** *Measure for Measure,* III, i, 40: Death makes these odds all even; *Cymbeline,* IV, ii, 263: Golden lads and girls all must, As chimney-sweepers, come to dust (see 97). **R.** 1732, Fuller.

Many deaths have place in men before they come to die. In the course of one's life, as one grows old, until eventually the time comes for one to die and reach the loss of everything, one has to suffer the deprivation of many pleasures, joys, interests. The words are from Gordon Bottomley's poem 'New Year's Eve, 1913'. They continue

> Joys must be used and spent, and then
> Abandoned and passed by.

Short debts (*or* reckonings) make long friends. *To pay promptly what one owes promotes lasting friendship* ('short' = 'paid in a short time'). This use of 'reckonings' is a survival of a meaning, which goes back to the fifteenth century, of 'settlement of accounts between parties'. Compare 'the day of reckoning' for the time when one will metaphorically pay, and will be punished, for one's misdeeds.

A. 1537: The commune prouerbe is that ofte [frequent] rekenings holdeth longe felawshyppe. Early variants from 'reckonings' were 'compting' (1641), 'counting' (1721), 'accounts' (1804); and a late nineteenth century one is 'debts'. I have heard also 'right' instead of 'short'.

79

Deeds, not words. *Words by themselves are of little or no value when it is action that is needed.* Often the phrase is used with reference to someone who is full of high-sounding but empty promises that lead to nothing. Sometimes the sentiment is expressed in a Latin form, *Facta non verba.* **A.** Chaucer: The wyse Plato seith, as ye may rede, The word mot nede accorde with the dede. 1616, Draxe: Doing is better than saying. Towards the end of the eighteenth century an anonymous poem was published that began 'A man of words and not of deeds, Is like a garden full of weeds.' **R.** 1812, Maria Edgeworth: 'Deeds not words' is my motto.

Compare **Fair words butter no parsnips (449).**

80

Every man has the defects of his qualities (*or* virtues). *Every good quality in a person has a corresponding weakness.* **R.** 1887.

The French have a phrase *Les défauts de ses qualités,* from which perhaps the English proverb originated.

81

The woman who deliberates (*or* hesitates) is lost. *A woman who, instead of at once rejecting (especially dishonourable) advances, deliberates whether to do so, will end by yielding.* 'hesitates' is the later form of the proverb. Its origin is Addison's *Cato* (IV, i, 29). In a variant sometimes heard or read 'The person' or 'He' is substituted for 'The woman', conveying an absurd condemnation of deliberation or hesitation in general.

82

Better the devil you know than the devil you don't. This is applied both to people and to things (including events,

[36]

troubles, misfortunes, etc.). **A.** (1) 1576, You had rather keep those whom you know, though with some faults, than take those whom you know not, perchance with more faults. (2) The dread of something after death . . . makes us rather bear those ills we have Than fly to others that we know not of (*Hamlet*, III, i, 81). **R.** 1857, Trollope, *Barchester Towers*. 1869, Hazlitt has 'harm' instead of 'devil'.

83

He should have (*or* He needs) a long spoon who sups with the devil. *A person must be on his guard when he enters into negotiations with a crafty scoundrel.* Chaucer: Therefore bihoueth him a ful long spoon that shal ete with a feend. The metaphor must have become and remained a familiar one, because two centuries later it is used by Shakespeare in one of the lighter scenes in the *Tempest*: This is a devil, and no monster; I will leave him; I have no long spoon.

84

Desperate diseases need (*or* must have) desperate cures (*or* remedies). *Serious evils need drastic remedies.* In Latin there was a proverb *Extremis malis extrema remedia* [For extreme evils there are extreme remedies]. Taverner, in his edition of Erasmus's *Adagia* (1539), has: Stronge disease requyreth a stronge medicine. Shakespeare in *Hamlet* (IV, iii, 9) has: Diseases desperate grown By desperate appliance are reliev'd, Or not at all; and two other adumbrations in *Romeo and Juliet* and *Much Ado about Nothing*. Defoe, 1713, has 'remedies' instead of 'cures'.

85

Fling dirt enough and some will stick. *If scurrilous abuse is profuse enough, some of it will find belief.* There was a Latin proverb, *Calumniare fortiter, aliquid adhaerebit*

[Calumniate violently, and something will stick]. *O.D.E.P.*
cites an adumbration in English in 1660 (by T. Hall, in
Funebria Florae): Lye lustily, some filth will stick; and in
1678, ascribed to Machiavelli, If durt enough be thrown,
some will stick. The proverb in its precisely current form
appears first in 1706 in E. Ward's *Hudibras Redivivus*:

> Scurrility's a useful trick,
> Approv'd by the most politic.
> Fling dirt enough, and some will stick.

86

Discretion is the better part of valour. A. 1477, Caxton:
Than as wyse and discrete he withdrewe him saying that
more is worth a good retrayte than a follishe abydinge.
Falstaff in *I Henry IV* (V, 14) says: The better part of valour
is discretion; in the which part I have saved my life. 1611,
Beaumont and Fletcher: It showed discretion the better part
of valour.

87

**There's a divinity that shapes our ends, rough-hew them
how we will.** *There is a heavenly power that ordains our lives,
whatever we do to shape them roughly and give them crude
form.* The words come from *Hamlet*, V, ii, 10.

88

Do as you would be done by. In *Matthew*, 7, 12, the word-
ing is: Therefore all things whatsoever ye would that men
should do to you, do ye even so to them; in *Luke* 6, 31: And
as ye would that men should do to you, do ye also to them
likewise. A common version of the sentiment is **Do unto
others as you would they should do unto you.**

[38]

Do as I say, not as I do. *Do not be deterred from following my advice because I fail in my conduct to carry out the principles I advocate.* **A.** 1546, Heywood: It is as folke dooe, and not as folke saie. **R.** 1689, Selden's *Table-talk*.

Apperson cites a French translation of a passage in Boccaccio (1313–75): *Faites ce que nous disons et ne faites pas ce que nous faisons* [Do what we say and not what we do].

Dog does not eat dog. In the current figurative use the meaning is that *one does not, or ought not to, attack, injure, try to profit from, a person of one's set, occupation, interests, cause.* Thus a doctor does not charge a fee to another doctor. In a literal sense the thought appears as early as in Juvenal in the first century B.C. about animals preying on their kind. Shakespeare in two plays says that bears do not bite one another. 1651, Herbert: A wolf will never make war upon another wolf. 1790, Wolcot: Dog should not prey on dog, the proverb says. **R.** 1866, C. Kingsley.

Every dog has his day. *At some stage in our lives we all have a period of success or prosperity or glory.* The first record of the proverb in its precisely present form is in Borrow's *Lavengro* (1851), but except for small variants, of 'a' instead of 'his', 'hath' instead of 'has', 'will have' instead of 'has', it is four centuries old. John Strype's *Ecclesiastical Memorials* records Princess (afterwards Queen) Elizabeth using the expression in a letter to her brother, Edward VI: As a dog hath a day, so may I perchance have time to declare it [my devotion to you] in deeds.

92

Give a dog a bad (*or* ill) name, and hang him. Figuratively, *if one succeeds in giving a person a bad reputation, it is easy to cause him to be regarded as guilty of any misconduct he is charged with.* The earliest date of the use of the expression is 1721 by Kelly, but there it is given a different interpretation from that with which it is used today: 'Spoken of those who raise an ill name on a man, on purpose to prevent his advancement'. **R.** 1760.

93

It is dogged that does it. *Success comes from perseverance and pertinacity.* 'dogged', having had primarily in Middle English the meaning merely of 'like a dog', 'canine', and later of 'cruel' or 'surly', came towards the end of the eighteenth century to mean 'obstinate', 'stubborn', 'pertinacious'. **R.** 1867, Trollope, in *Last Chronicles of Barset*, Mr. Crawley repeated Giles Hoggett's words: 'It's dogged that does it. It's not thinking about it.'

94

Let sleeping dogs lie. Figuratively, *Do not disturb a state of affairs that at present is dormant, causing no trouble, but has potentialities for harm if interfered with.* Compare **Leave (*or* Let) well alone (225).** Chaucer, *The Franklin's Tale*: Lat slepen that is stille [Let sleep that which is still]; *Troylus and Criseyde*: It is nought good a slepying hound to wake. **R.** 1824, Scott.

95

Dreams go by contraries. 1673, Wycherley: Dreams go by the contraries.

[40]

A drowning man will clutch (*or* catch) at a straw. Figuratively, *a person in desperate straits will put his hope on, or seize every chance, however slight or improbable, to extricate himself from danger or difficulty.* The metaphor appears in Latin in a letter by Seneca, of which an English translation was published in 1650. 1612, Bishop J. Hall: The drowning man snatches at every twig. **R.** 1748, in Richardson's *Clarissa Harlowe.*

Golden lads and girls all must, as chimney-sweepers, come to dust. This is from the song in *Cymbeline*, by Guiderius and Arviragus beginning (IV, ii)

> Fear no more the heat o' the sun,
>   Nor the furious winter's rages,
> Thou thy worldly task hast done,
>   Home art gone and ta'en thy wages.

Compare **Death is the grand leveller** (76).

Early to bed and early to rise makes a man healthy, wealthy and wise. A. 1523: Erly rysing maketh a man hole in body, holer in soule, and rycher in goodes. **R.** Ray, 1670.

The early bird catches the worm. The proverb goes back to 1605. *O.D.E.P.* gives no record of the figurative use, which is the only sense in which it is used now, meaning that *in an enterprise, competition, application, success comes to the person who, to use another metaphor, is early in the field.*

[41]

100

(a) **Easy,** (b) **Light** (*or* **Lightly**), (c) **Quickly, come; easy etc., go.** All the versions are current and have the same meaning, that *advantages, benefits, profits, gained, or falling to one's lot without effort are equally easily and quickly spent or lost.*

(a) is not recorded until the nineteenth century. (b) **A.** *c.* 1387, Chaucer: And lightly as it comth so wol we spende. **R.** 1546, Heywood. (c) **A.** 1583, Melbanke: Quickly spent thats easely gotten; 1631, Mabbe: Quickly be wonne, and quickly be lost. **R.** 1869, Hazlitt.

101

One cannot eat one's cake and have it. (Mr. Eric Partridge in his *Dictionary of Clichés* mentions that this maxim is often incorrectly expressed **One cannot have one's cake and eat it.**) Figuratively, *one cannot reap the advantages of two opposed courses of conduct.* Thus one cannot indulge in the pleasure of spending money freely and at the same time enjoy the satisfaction of saving money. 1546, Heywood: Wolde ye bothe eate your cake and have your cake? 1611, Davies, *The Scourge of Folly*: A man cannot eat his cake and have it still.

Compare **You cannot have it both ways** (28).

102

Eheu fugaces. *Alas the flying* (*years*). The full Latin phrase, from an ode by Horace, is *Eheu fugaces labuntur anni* [Alas the flying years roll by].

Compare **Time flies** (409).

103

The end crowns all (*or* **the work**). *It is the final result that completes all that went before and is its culmination.* The

words are a translation of a Latin maxim *Finis coronat opus.*
A. 1592, Kyd: The end is crown of every work well done. **R.**
Shakespeare's *Troilus and Cressida*, IV, v.

104

Look to (*or* Mark) the end. *Take thought of what the end
will be.* This is a translation of the Latin phrase *Respice
finem.* The thought, however, goes back much further,
being expressed by Chilon, one of the 'Wise Men' of
Greece, about 600 B.C. **A.** *Cursor Mundi,* 1300: For qua
bigin wil ani thing He aght to thinc on the ending [For however anything begins, one ought to think about the ending].
1550, Latimer: *Respice finem,* mark the end; look upon the
end.

105

Better an open enemy than a false friend. A. 1200: Ueond
thet thuncheð freond is swike ouer alle swike [An enemy
who seems a friend is of all traitors the most treacherous].
Richard III (III, i, 16): God keep me from false friends.
R. 1655, Gurnall: A false friend is worse than an open
enemy in man's judgment; and a hypocritical Judas more
abhorred by God than a bloody Pilate. 1727, Gay: An open
foe may be a curse, But a pretended friend is worse.

106

The way to an Englishman's heart is through his stomach.
1845, Ford, *Handbook for Travellers in Spain*: The way
to many an honest heart lies through the belly. 1857, Mrs.
Craik, *John Halifax, Gentleman* (no doubt regarding 'belly'
as too vulgar a word to use): There's a saying that the way
to an Englishman's heart is through his stomach. She
is the only writer to particularise the Englishman.

[43]

107

Enough is as good as a feast. 1420, Lydgate: As good ys ynough as a gret feste. **R.** Heywood, 1546. Lamb, in *Popular Fallacies*, calls the saying a 'cold-scrag-of-mutton Sophism; a lie palmed upon the palate, which knows better things'.

108

To err is human. There was a Latin saying exactly equivalent to this, *humanum errare*. **A.** (1) 1542, Udall, in a translation of Erasmus's collection of classical proverbs: Bothe wer men, and might err. (2) In 1575 another translation, from a book written in Latin, has 'Tullie [Cicero] sayth to err is man's propertie'. **R.** 1711, Pope (*Essay on Criticism*): To err is human, to forgive divine.

109

Every man for himself and the devil take the hindmost. *These are circumstances, or This is a case, where everyone must look after his own interests, and those who are weak, incompetent, indolent, must come to disaster.* **A.** 1514: Eche man for him selfe, and the fiende for all. 1572: Every man for self, and the Devill for all. The earliest date for the record of the saying in its current form (given within quotation marks, i.e. as a recognised proverb) is 1858.

110

Every man is the architect of his own fortunes. This is a translation of an older statement in Latin quoted supposedly by Sallust in the first century B.C. In English literature Udall in 1533 quotes another Latin maxim that he translates as Every man maketh, is causer of his own fortunes. 1539, Taverner: A man's owne maners do shape hym hys fortune.

In the seventeenth century there are variants of 'workman', 'artificer', 'architect', 'smith'. **R.** 1873, a writer in *Notes and Queries* cites the proverb as one of our most common sayings.

111

Evil communications corrupt good manners. *Association with bad people ruins a person's morals.* (For the sense of 'manners' see **Manners makyth man,** 259.) The proverb is adopted from *I Corinthians*, 15, 33. That in its turn may have been suggested to the translator of the Bible by his knowledge of a corresponding Greek proverb attributed to the ancient Greek poet Menander.

112

For every evil under the sun there is a remedy or there is none. If there is one, try to find it; if there is not, never mind it. Carew Hazlitt's *Proverbs*, 1869.

113

Of two evils choose the less (*or* the least). Variants in early records for 'evils' are 'ills', 'harms', 'mischief'; and for 'less' are 'least', 'lesser', 'smallest'. *c.* 1380, Chaucer: Of harmes two the lesse is for to chese. **R.** Heywood, 1546.

114

Example is better than precept. *To practise what one says ought to be done is more effective in gaining results than merely to enjoin it.* **A.** 1400: Then saythe Seynt Austeyn that on ensampull yn doying ys mor commendabull than yn techyng other [or] preechyng. **R.** 1824: D. Moir, *Mansie Wauch.*

[45]

115

The exception proves the rule is a translation of a medieval Latin aphorism, *Exceptio probat regulam.* The English form taken in the present sense of 'proves' makes nonsense, but 'probat', in Latin, and 'proves' in English as at one time used: e.g. in the Authorised Version of the Bible, mean 'tests'; and the meaning of the statement is that an exception compels the re-examination of the validity of a rule or generalisation.

116

Exchange (*or* A fair exchange) is no robbery. A. 1546, Heywood: Chaunge be no robry, but robry makeith chaunge. **R.** 1662, Fuller (the divine).

117

Blessed is he who expects nothing, for he shall never be disappointed. This comes from a letter by Pope to John Gay (1727).

118

He who excuses himself accuses himself. St. Jerome (third century A.D.): *Dum excusare credis, accusas* [While you believe you excuse, you accuse]. French (1575): *Qui s'excuse s'accuse.* **A.** 1616, Draxe: To excuse is to accuse.

119

Extremes meet. *Among people and things that in a general way or in most ways are the opposite to each other there is sometimes one element that is the same.* Thus a communist and a conservative may be identical, may correspond, may figuratively 'meet', each showing great enthusiasm for his cause, though in detailed aims and principles devoted to extreme contraries.

The earliest record of the saying is in Walpole's *Letters* (1780). Charles Lamb in *Chimney-sweepers* (1822) has 'That dead time of the dawn, when (as extremes meet) the rake . . . and the hard-handed artisan jostle'.

120

That is all my eye. *That is all nonsense, humbug.* **R.** 1768, Goldsmith. It has been conjectured that the expression referred originally to the tears of a person affecting emotion he does not feel; the tears are in his eye, but do not spring from his heart.

There is a later and longer form, **That is all (in) my eye and Betty Martin.** The origin of this is unknown. Joe Miller, the eighteenth-century humorist, invented a farcical story that a British sailor, going into a foreign church, heard someone saying, '*O mihi, beate Martine*' meaning 'O grant me aid, blessed St. Martin'; and, giving an account of this, said it sounded like 'All my eye and Betty Martin'.

121

What the eye does not see the heart does not grieve. *If one does not, literally see, figuratively know of, a thing, one is not unhappy about it.* ('grieve' here = 'grieve at or for'. The verb was so used in the sixteenth century.)

This is, I think, the most common current form of the saying, with the word 'grieve'. *O.D.E.P.*, however, gives it only with the verb 'rue', and records it as so cited by Taverner (1539), in a neat epigram: That the eye seeth not, ye herte rueth not. Some people may read the proverb to mean 'Shut your eyes to the suffering of others', a lesson of doubtful morality.

122

Four eyes see more (*or* better) than two. Latin proverb, *Plus vident oculi quam oculus* [Eyes see more than one eye]. **A.** 1599, Minsheu, *A Spanish Grammar*: Four eies see better then two. Bacon, 1594, has: Two eyes are better than one. **R.** 1898, Max Müller.

123

Facilis descensus Averni. *The path down to evil is easy.* (The correct Latin is *Averno*.) The words come from an account in Virgil's *Aeneid*, VI, 126, of the descent to hell. It is followed by a description of the contrasting difficulty of retracing one's steps and reaching the upper air (i.e., applied figuratively to regaining the paths of virtue).

124

Fact (*or* Truth) is stranger than fiction. The earliest record of the statement about Fact is in 1881, in a book called *Arcady*, by A. Jessopp; about Truth, fifty-eight years earlier, by Byron, in *Don Juan* (XIV, ci).

125

Facts are stubborn things. *Facts are undeniable realities that are not to be got over, got rid of, ignored, conquered, by wishes or theories.* **R.** 1749, Smollett's translation of Le Sage's *Gil Blas*.

126

Faint heart never won fair lady. **A.** 1569: Faint hearts faire ladies neuer win. **R.** Camden, 1614. Compare Dryden, 'Alexander's Feast', 1687: None but the brave deserve the fair.

All is fair in love and war. A. (1) 1606: An old saw hath
bin, Faith's breach for love and kingdoms is no sin. (2)
1630, Beaumont and Fletcher: All stratagems in love, and
that the sharpest war, are lawful. In 1801 Maria Edgeworth
too uses the phrase, 'every stratagem' as being 'fair in love
and war'. R. 1850, Smedley, *Frank Fairlegh*.

A proverb adumbrated by a cynic, and repeated by
generations of cynics. Every article in the Geneva con-
vention against cruelty in warfare contradicts the second
part of it.

The falling-out of lovers is the renewing of love. The origin
of the sentiment is in the play *Andria* of the Latin playwright
Terence. Its first record in English literature, in its current
form, is in Burton's *Anatomy of Melancholy* (1621), as a
translation of Terence's words. 1847, Tennyson, *The Princess*: Blessings on the falling out That all the more endears.

A variant of the sentiment refers, not to lovers, but to
friends. 1566, Edwardes, *Paradise of Dainty Deuises*: The
falling out of faithful friends renuing is of love; and this is
a translation of the Latin of Terence, *amantium* being
translated 'friends'.

Familiarity breeds contempt. There is an expression of
this sentiment in Latin literature by Publilius Syrus. Chaucer:
Men seyn that 'over-greet homlinesse engendreth disprey-
singe'. R. 1654, Fuller (the divine), who, however, says
this happens only in 'base and sordid natures'. But Trollope, *He knew He was right*, has: 'Perhaps, if I heard
Tennyson talking every day, I shouldn't read Tennyson.
Familiarity does breed contempt'. Compare **No man is a
hero to his valet** (180).

130

The farthest (*or* longest) way round (*or* about) is the nearest (*or* shortest) way home. Literally, *what seems a long and roundabout route gets one to a destination more quickly than a short and direct one.* Figuratively, *a short and direct method of doing a thing, which is thought will gain an object quickly or easily, is less effective than a long and indirect one.* **R.** 1661, Robert Boyle.

131

Fast (*or* Safe, *or* Sure) bind, fast, etc., find. *If a thing is put away securely, it will be quickly found.* There is a pun on 'fast', which is used to mean first 'firmly' and then 'quickly'. **A.** Caxton, 1494: Who that well byndeth wel can be unbound? **R.** Heywood, 1546. Shakespeare uses it, quoting it as a proverb, in *The Merchant of Venice* (II, v).

132

Like father, like son. The origin of this statement is the corresponding Latin words of Athanasius (296–373). It is quoted, in its Latin form, by Langland, 1377. 1509, Barclay: An olde prouerbe hath longe agone be sayde That oft the sone in måner lyke wyll be Vnto the Father. This is followed by the statement: The mayde, or daughter, vnto the mother wyll agre. In 1616 Draxe too has: **Like father like sonne; like mother like daughter.** But the comparison between mother and daughter has not become common, though it appears in *Ezekiel*, 16, 44.

133

Fiat justitia, ruat coelum. *Justice must be done even if the sky falls*: i.e. at all costs, whatever dreadful results may follow. The expression does not appear in classical Latin. Mr. Eric Partridge, in his *Dictionary of Clichés*, cites the words of St. Augustine (345–430), *Fiat jus et pereat mundus* [Let right be done, and let the world perish], and says the saying came into use in the seventeenth century. **R.** 1603, William Watson.

134

He who fights and runs away may live to fight another day. The origin of the saying was an ancient Greek proverbial verse, that the man who flees will fight again. It must not, however, be interpreted as encouraging cowardice.

The orator Demosthenes, when reproached with having run away at the battle of Chaeronea, 338 B.C., laughingly quoted the words. In English we find, as early as 1250: Wel fytht that wel flyth. There is a tendency to run into rhyme. 1542, Udall, translating Erasmus's *Adagia*: That same man, that renneth awaie, Maie again fight an other daie; and 1663, Butler's *Hudibras*: For those that fly may fight again, Which he can never do that's slain. 1750, Ray, has 'turn and' instead of 'live to'. **R.** 1849.

135

Fine feathers make fine birds. In early records (where 'Fine' is 'Fair', and 'birds' is 'fowls') the saying is used without irony to mean, as Ray, 1679, puts it: Fair clothes, ornaments, and dresses set off persons. Today, however, it is generally used to mean that fine clothes often cover only a bad character, stupidity, etc.

136

First impressions are half the battle (*or* are most lasting). Dickens's *Martin Chuzzlewit*: First impressions, you know, go a long way, and last a long time. I have not found a printed record of the current form of the proverb.

[51]

137

There are as good fish in the sea as ever came out of it.
Figuratively, *There is no need to despair of coming across
something equally good.* **R.** 1822, Scott, *The Fortunes of
Nigel*; and 1881, Gilbert, in *Patience* has

> There's fish in the sea, no doubt of it,
> As good as ever came out of it.

138

Big fleas have little fleas. *We all, big and small, important
and insignificant, have people or things to trouble us.* 'big' is
a misquotation for 'great' from the lines by Augustus de
Morgan, in *A Budget of Paradoxes* (1872)

> Great fleas have little fleas upon their backs to bite
>   'em.
> And little fleas have lesser fleas, and so *ad in-
>   finitum.*

But this was clearly adapted from Swift's lines, 'On
Poetry'

> So, naturalists observe, a flea
> Hath smaller fleas that on him prey;
> And these have smaller fleas to bite 'em,
> And so proceed *ad infinitum.*
> Thus every poet, in his kind,
> Is bit by him that comes behind.

139

Many a flower is born to blush unseen. *Many people never
have their beauties and virtue recognised.* From Gray's
Elegy written in a Country Churchyard. The verse continues,
And waste its sweetness on the desert air.

140

A fool and his money are soon parted. *A foolish person soon spends all his money.* **A.** Tusser, 1573: A foole and his monie be soone at debate, Which after with sorrow repents him too late. **R.** 1629, Howell.

141

There is no fool like an old fool. *A person who is old when he commits follies runs to worse excesses than the young.* Heywood, 1546: There is no foole to the olde foole, folke says. For three centuries the form of the saying retained 'to', until Tennyson in *The Grandmother* (1852) wrote 'Ah, there's no fool like the old one'.

142

A fool's bolt is soon shot. *A foolish person soon gets to the end of any plan or resource he has.* 1300: Sottes bolt is sone i-schote. **R.** Shakespeare, *Henry V*, III, vii.

143

Forbidden fruit is sweet. A. 1628: But as the proverb hath it, apples are sweet when they are plucked in the gardener's absence. **R.** 1855, in Bohn's *Handbook of Proverbs*.
Compare **Stolen waters are sweet** (393).

144

Forewarned (is) forearmed. A. 1530, Hills, *Commonplace Books*: He that is warned ys half armed. **R.** 1592.

145

**Fortune knocks once at least at every man's gate (*or* door).
A.** 1567: Fortune once in the course of our life dothe put

into our handes the offer of a good torne. **R.** 1869, in
W. C. Hazlitt's *English Proverbs and Proverbial Phrases.*

146

A friend to all (*or* **everybody**) **is a friend to none** (*or* **nobody**). The ancient Greeks had a saying, originating in
Aristotle's *Ethics*, and repeated five or six centuries later by
Diogenes Laertius, that 'to him to whom there are friends
there is no friend'. In English literature the thought is first
recorded in 1623: All men's friend, no man's friend.

147

A friend in need is a friend indeed. A. (1) 1270: A such
fere the his help in mode [A safe companion is he that helps
at need]. (2) R. Barnfield, *The Passionate Pilgrim*: He that
is thy friend indeed, he will help thee in thy need. **R.** 1678,
Ray.

148

God defend (*or* **deliver,** *or* **preserve**) **me from my friends.**
1477, Rivers: Ther was one that praied god to kepe him
from the daunger of his friends. **R.** 1604, Marston: Now God
deliver me from my friends . . . for from my enemies Ile
deliver myself. 1850, Charlotte Brontë: I can be on my
guard against my enemies, but God deliver me from my
friends. Lockhart quotes Scott as saying the origin of the
saying was Spanish. The proverb obviously is not a warning
against friendship; one may read perhaps 'well-meaning but
blundering friends'.

149

By their fruits ye shall know them. This saying (always
used figuratively) comes from *Matthew*, 7, 20. There is a
[54]

corresponding proverb, less common, also from *Matthew* (12, 33): **A tree is known by its fruit.**

150

Gather ye rosebuds while ye may. *Get what pleasures and joys you can while you are still young.* The words come from a poem by Herrick (1648), in which, under the title 'Counsel to Girls' (later 'To the Virgins, to make much of Time'), there is an injunction to 'be not coy, but use your time; And while ye may, go marry.'

151

Do not look a gift horse in the mouth. *Do not examine a present too critically.* This is an adaptation of the Latin words of St. Jerome (A.D. 386), *Noli equi dentes inspicere donati* [Do not examine the teeth of a horse that has been given you]. A horse's age is judged by the state of its teeth.

St. Jerome in his turn must have been citing a proverb, because he writes *ut vulgare proverbium est* [as the common proverb says]. Professor Watt tells me there was not one in ancient Latin, or in ancient Greek except one by Zenobius: Whatever the gift anyone gives, commend it.

A. 1539, Taverner: A gyuen [given] hors maye not be loked in the mouthe.

The saying is one of the 'Popular Fallacies' in the essays of Lamb, who says in caustic vein: 'Some people have a knack of putting upon you gifts of no real value, to engage you to substantial gratitude. We thank them for nothing'.

152

It is more blessed to give than to receive. This is from *Acts* 20, 35.

[55]

153

Those who live in glass houses should not throw stones. Figuratively, *One should not accuse others of faults that oneself commits.* A. Chaucer writes of a person with a head of glass who throws stones in war. 1640, Herbert: Whose house is of glass must not throw stones at another.

154

The paths of glory lead but to the grave. *The career of even the most successful and illustrious person ends in death.* This comes from Gray's *Elegy written in a Country Churchyard*, ix.

155

God's mill grinds (*or* mills grind) slow but sure. *Divine retribution often takes a long time in reaching a malefactor, but, when it comes, it awards condign punishment.* The metaphor appears in classical Greek in the form: The mills of the gods grind slowly but they grind small. 'small' too appears in an often-quoted expression of the thought by Longfellow, in a translation of a German poem: Though the mills of God grind slowly, yet they grind exceeding small.

156

God's in his heaven; all's right with the world. This is from the first of Pippa's four songs in Browning's *Pippa Passes* (1841). Pippa's philosophy is that of a girl waking at dawn on a rare holiday. As a basis for human conduct the second half of the line is hardly adequate.

God (*or* **Heaven**) **helps them who help themselves.** The Romans had a proverb *Dii facientes adjuvant*, which Taverner, 1545, translates: The goddes do helpe the doers. 1611, Cotgrave: Begin to help thy selfe, and God will help thee. **R.** 1736, Benjamin Franklin.

Whom the gods love die young. This is a translation of a sentiment expressed in classical Greek by Menander (342–291 B.C.), and in classical Latin by Plautus (254–184 B.C.), who adds 'while still enjoying health, feeling, and understanding'. In English literature the earliest reference to the thought is in 1546, Wilson, *Arte of Rhetorique*: Whom God loueth best, those he taketh sonest. **R.** Byron, *Don Juan*. In 1923 E. V. Lucas writes that it has never been satisfactorily determined whether the saying about the darlings of the gods dying young means young in years or young in heart.

All is not gold that glitters. Figuratively, *Fine outward appearances are often delusive, and cloak what is of no value.* The Romans had a proverb *Non omne quod nitet aurum est* [Not everything that shines is gold]. 1220, *Nis hit nower neh gold al that ter schineth* [Nor is all that shines there anything like gold]. From 1300 there are records of the image with slight variants. The verb in the adjectival clause is at first 'shineth'; then 'glistereth', 'glisters' (e.g. *The Merchant of Venice*, II, vii, 65), 'glittereth'. **R.** 1553.

The good is the enemy of the best: see **The best is often the enemy of the good** (15).

161

One good turn deserves (or asks, or requires) another.
1400: O good turne asket another. **R.** 1550, Heywood.

162

There is nothing either good or bad but thinking makes it so. This is a quotation from *Hamlet*, II, ii. It is Hamlet's cynical rejoinder to Rosencrantz, who has been praising Denmark, equivalent to 'Well, that's what you think'.

163

Grasp all, lose all. *In greedily trying to get everything or too much, you will, or may, fail to get anything, and lose what you have.* **A.** 1205: For the mon is muchel sot: the nimeo to himseoluen Mare thonne he mazen walde [For the man is a great fool who taketh upon himself more than he can manage]. Chaucer: For the proverbe seith He that to muche embraceth distreyneth [gets into his possession] litel. The reference may be to Æsop's fable of the dog that, trying to seize a reflection of a bone it sees in the water, loses what it has in its mouth. **R.** 1790.
Compare **Catch not at the shadow and lose the substance** (375).

164

When Greek meets Greek, then comes the tug of war. *It is when champions or leading opponents on both sides enter a contest, that the great struggle or test comes.* This is a perversion of 'When Greeks join'd Greeks then was the tug of war' from a play by Nathaniel Lee in the latter part of the seventeenth century.

[58]

A green Christmas (*or* **Yule,** *or* **winter) makes a full** (*or* **fat) churchyard. A.** 1635: A hot Christmas makes a fat churchyard. **R.** 1670, Ray. 1721, Kelly, in citing the proverb, adds 'This, and a great many proverbial observations upon the seasons of the year, are groundless'.

Half a loaf is better than no bread. *To possess half or a substantial part of what one desires is so much better than to have none that it should make one moderately satisfied.* 1546, Heywood. The French have a saying, *Faut de grives on mange des merles* [When one lacks thrushes one eats blackbirds].

Many hands make light (*or* **quick,** *or* **slight) work.** 1350: Many hondys makyn lyght worke.
Contrast **Too many cooks spoil the broth** (59).

Handsome is that (*or* **as,** *or* **who) handsome does.** *It is a person's conduct that merits admiration.* The expression is a play on the word 'handsome' in its two senses of what in a person's appearance is pleasing to the eye, and what in his conduct is admirable.
A. 1580: Goodly is he that goodly dooth. 1600: He is proper that proper doth. 1670, Ray: He is handsome that handsome doth. **R.** 1766, Goldsmith, *The Vicar of Wakefield.*
The proverb is dealt with in the 'Popular Fallacies' of Lamb, who, however, uses it only to elaborate the thesis that 'true ugliness, no less than is affirmed of true beauty, is the result of harmony'.

169

As good (*or* well) be hanged for a sheep as a lamb. *Since one is about to do what is bound to get one into trouble, one may as well, while one is about it, go for something big.* 1578, Ray: As good be hang'd for an old sheep as a young lamb. The allusion is to the time when hanging was a punishment for sheep-stealing.

170

Happy is the country that has no history. *That no events have happened needing chronicle means that the country has had a calm, peaceful existence free of troubles, disturbances, adversity, tragedies.* O.D.E.P. cites Carlyle in *Frederick the Great* (1858–65): Happy the people whose annals are blank in history. Carlyle quotes this from Montesquieu with, translated, 'history-books' instead of 'history'.

171

Call no man happy until he is dead (*or* dies). This means, not that it is better to be dead than alive, as, for example, Hardy said ('The dead are the best off'), but that *we cannot justifiably regard any person as having a happy life until he is dead because, while he is alive, however happy he may be and have been, up to a given moment, misfortune and unhappiness may still happen to him.* The thought found frequent expression among classical writers, especially, in prose, by Herodotus, in the account of Croesus related by Solon; and, in poetry, by Aeschylus, Sophocles, Euripides, Ovid. In English an adumbration of the thought appears in 1603 in Florio's translation of Montaigne

> We must expect of man the latest day,
> Nor e'er he die, he's happy, can we say.

The earliest record of the sentiment in its current form is not given by *O.D.E.P.* before the end of the nineteenth century.

A similar thought was expressed in 1539 in a less common and current form by Taverner, first in Latin, quoting Erasmus, *Vitae finem specta* [Look at the end of life], and then in translation expanded to **Praise no man for blessed and happy till thou se the ende of his life.**

Three centuries later an adaptation of this use of the word 'praise' took the form of **Praise no man till he is dead** in a play by Robert Louis Stevenson and his wife, *The Hanging Judge*, written in 1887, but not published till 1914, twenty years after Stevenson's death.

172

(The) more haste, (the) less (*or* worse) speed. *Often in trying to hurry one ends by taking more time or making less progress than if one had gone leisurely.* **R.** 1350. Skeat, in *A Student's Pastime*, citing the proverb, writes: 'When we remember that "speed" meant "success" in Old English, the sense becomes "The more haste, the worse success", which is a perfectly wise and sensible saying'.

173

Make haste slowly. There is a classical Greek origin of this phrase, and a Latin one (*Festina lente*, attributed by Suetonius to Augustus). Chaucer: He hasteth wel that wisly can abide. **R.** 1744, Benjamin Franklin.

174

Make hay while the sun shines. Figuratively, *Press on with the job, or seize every advantage you can, while conditions are favourable.* **A.** 1509, Barclay: Who that in July whyle Phebus is shyngnge About his hay is nat besy labourynge Shall in the wynter his negligence bewayle. 1546, Heywood: Whan the sunne shinth make hay. **R.** 1583, Melbancke. Trench, writing in 1852, says: 'Make hey while the sun shines' is truly English, and could have had its birth only under such variable skies as ours.

175

Two (*or* Many) heads are better than one. A. 1390, Gower: Two han more wit than on. **R.** 1546, Heywood.
An extension of the proverb sometimes heard is, after 'one', **even if the one's a sheep's.** In folk-phrase a sheep's head means a daft or unreasoning head. A sheep is traditionally regarded as a foolish creature.

176

Kind hearts are more than coronets. *There is more virtue in having a gentle sympathetic nature than in being high-born and bearing a title of nobility.* The words come from Tennyson's 'Lady Clara Vere de Vere'. They continue 'And simple faith than Norman blood'.

177

It is a poor heart that never rejoices. 1833, Marryat, *Peter Simple*; 1843, Dickens, *Martin Chuzzlewit*. 'poor' here seems to mean 'cheerless', 'dispirited', 'miserable', 'unhappy'.

178

Hell has no fury like a woman scorned. ('scorned' = 'whose love has been rejected'.) This is an adaptation of Congreve's *Mourning Bride* (III, viii)

> Heav'n has no rage like love to hatred turn'd,
> Nor Hell a fury like a woman scorn'd.

[62]

Mr. Eric Partridge in his *Dictionary of |Clichés* suggests that Congreve may have drawn the idea from Fletcher in *The Knight of Malta* ('The wages of scorn'd love is baneful hate'), or Cibber in *Love's Last Shift* ('We shall find no fiend in hell can match the fury of a disappointed woman—scorned, slighted, dismissed').

179

Hell is paved with good intentions. *Sin is often preceded by good resolutions.* Mr. Burton Stevenson ascribes the origin of the idea to Bernard of Clairvaux (*c.* 1150), and mentions several adumbrations in English from the fifteenth century. *O.D.E.P.* records the sentiment as first found in Wesley's *Journals* (1736). Pearsall Smith says the idea of hell being paved was adapted from the Spanish by Richard Baxter (1651). Strictly it is the road leading to hell, not hell itself, that one would regard as paved with intentions not executed.

180

No man is a hero to his valet. A. 1685, translated by Charles Cotton from Montaigne: Few men have been admired by their domestics. 1764, Foote: It has been said that no man is a hero to his *valet de chambre*. *O.D.E.P.* does not give a record of the proverb in its current form. **Ot.** now that valets are obsolete or rare.

181

History repeats itself. Mr. Burton Stevenson derives the expression from the Greek of Thucydides, which he gives in translation as 'I shall be content if those shall pronounce my History useful who desire to give a view of events as they really happened, and as they are very likely in accordance with human nature to repeat themselves at some future time—if not exactly the same, yet very similar.'
R. 1885, A. Jessopp.

[63]

182

Hitch your wagon to a star. *Follow a lofty principle to guide you in all you do.* The maxim is from an essay by Emerson (1870).

183

Home is home, though it be never so homely. 'homely' here means 'plain', 'simple'. **R.** 1670, Ray. Compare the next two proverbs.

The proverb appears in the 'Popular Fallacies' of Lamb, who uses it to describe 'homes that are no homes; the home of the very poor man, . . . with shivering children, . . . the clamours of a wife, . . . no larder, . . . no visitors, . . . senseless and impertinent news', contrasted with the cheerfulness of an inn.

184

There is no place like home. This comes from a song by J. H. Payne, 1822:

> Mid pleasures and palaces though we may roam,
> Be it ever so humble, there's no place like home . . .
> Home, home, sweet, sweet home!
> There's no place like home! there's no place
> like home!

Compare the last proverb and the next.

185

East or West, home is best. 1855, Bohn's *Handbook of Proverbs.*

Compare the last two proverbs.

Even Homer sometimes nods. *Even the greatest writer sometimes makes a mistake.* The statement is a translation of Horace's words in *Ars Poetica*. The first record of it in English literature is in 1530. **R.** 1674, Dryden.

Honesty is the best policy. The expression is recorded as first used in 1599 by G. Sandys. **R.** Cotgrave, 1611, and Ray, 1670, cite a contrary statement, **The honester man the worse luck.**

Honi soit qui mal y pense. This is the Norman-French form, still used by us, of the motto that translated literally says *Disgraced may he be who thinks (or seeks or plans) ill (or evil)*; and sometimes given as *Ill be to (or Shame take) him that thinketh ill.* It is the motto of the Order of the Garter. **A.** 1386, Chaucer: Yvel shall have that yvel wol deserve. 1484, Caxton: Now the euyl which men wysshe to other cometh to hym whiche wysseth hit. **R.** 1712, Motteux, in translation of *Don Quixote*: Evil to him that evil seeks.

honnir (two n's in modern spelling), 'to disgrace', is one of the few words in French where *h* is aspirated.

Honour to whom honour is due. *Honour should be given where (or when) it is due.* I have not been able to find records of the earlier use of this expression. But *Romans*, 13, 7, Authorised Version, has: Render therefore to all their dues: tribute to whom tribute is due; custom to whom custom; fear to whom fear; honour to whom honour.

190

There is honour among thieves. The first record of an adumbration of the proverb in English is in 1712 in a translation of *Don Quixote*: The old [Spanish] proverb still holds good, 'Thieves are never rogues among themselves'. But over a century earlier Shakespeare (*I Henry IV*, II, ii) has: 'A plague upon it when thieves cannot be true one to another'. R. 1828, Bulwer Lytton, *Pelham*.

191

Hope deferred makes *or* maketh the heart sick. This comes from the Bible, Authorised and Revised Versions, *Proverbs*, 13, 12. Wycliff's translation in 1382, over two centuries earlier, had: Hope that is defferid tormenteth the soule.

192

Hope springs eternal. These are the first words in a couplet in Pope's *Essay on Man*

> Hope springs eternal in the human breast;
> Man never is, but always to be, blest.

193

Without (*or* If it were not for) hope, the heart would break. 1220: Ase me seith, zif hope nere, heorte to breke [As men say, if there was no hope, the heart would break]. R. 1614, Camden.

194

He who has a wife and children has given hostages to fortune. The thought is expressed by the Latin poet Lucan (A.D. 39–65): *Conjunx est mihi, sunt nati; dedimus tot pignora fatis* [I have a wife; we have children; such pledges we have given to fate]. 1612, Bacon's *Essays*: He that hath Wife, and Children, hath given Hostages to Fortune, for they are Impediments to great Enterprises.

We must not of course take the proverb as discouraging marriage and paternity.

195

One crowded hour of glorious life is worth an age without a name. This comes from a quatrain by Mordaunt (1730–1809), popularised by Scott's quotation of it in *Old Mortality* (1815).

196

A man's (*or* an Englishman's) house is his castle. A. 1581: The English papists owe it to the Queen that youre house is youre Castell. 1642, Fuller (the divine): It was wont to be said A man's House is his castle. 1779, Dr. Johnson: A man's own house is truly his *castle*, in which he can be in perfect safety from intrusion.

197

Hunger is the best sauce. This goes back in ancient Greek to Socrates, reported by Xenophon, Cicero and others, as saying that hunger was a sauce for seasoning food (in Cicero's words *cibi condimentum esse famem*). In 1362 Langland writes of 'hunger sending its sauce'. In 1542 Udall, in a translation of Erasmus's *Adagia*, quotes the statement attributed to Socrates. The date of the first record of the saying in its current English form is 1555 in R. Eden's *Decades*.

198

Idle folks have the least leisure. R. 1853, Surtees. Compare **Busiest men have the most time (34).**

[67]

199

Where ignorance is bliss, 'tis folly to be wise. *If knowledge brings only disillusion and pain, one is better ignorant.* The words are the last line in Gray's 'Ode on a Distant Prospect of Eton College'. Gray is referring to the carefree days of schoolboys who do not know about the evils future life has in store for them. 'A pernicious maxim' has been the charge made against the sentiment by an austere annotator of the poem, 'which ignores the fact that blissful ignorance is often the cause of disaster, and that an accession of wisdom may add to the bliss the ignorant had felt'.

200

(1) There is no ill in life that is not worse without bread. (2) All sorrows are less with bread. (1) *Every trouble is worse if one has no money.* (2) *Every trouble is better if one has money.* These are variants of a remark in *Don Quixote* (1605) by Sancho Panza. Herbert, 1640: All griefs with bread are less.

201

Ill weeds grow apace (*or* fast). Literally, *the worse a particular sort of weed is, the quicker it grows and spreads.* Figuratively, *bad things spread quickly and far (with the implication of more quickly and further than good things).* 1470: Wyld weed ys sone y-growe. 1546, Heywood: Ill weede growth fast. *Richard III* (II, iv): Sweet flowers are slow and weeds make haste. **R.** 1614, Camden ('fast'); 1660, Tatham ('apace').

202

It's an ill wind that blows nobody good (*or* any good). Figuratively, *it is seldom that a misfortune does not benefit*

[68]

someone or something. 1546, Heywood: An yll wynde that bleuth no man to good, men say.

203

Ill-gotten goods never prosper. *Things gained dishonestly never bring lasting benefit.* The thought is expressed by the early Greek poet Hesiod: Dishonest gains are losses; and in Latin by Cicero, translated by Taverner (1539): Euyl gotten good go euyl awaye. From the sixteenth to the eighteenth century there are records of the proverb with variants of the verbal phrase: 'never prove long', 'little time endure', 'have bad success', 'never thrive', 'are ill gone'.

The proverb (with 'gain' instead of 'goods') appears in Lamb's *Popular Fallacies* (1826). Lamb describes it as 'the trite consolation administered to the easy dupe, when he has been tricked out of his money or estate, that the acquisition of it will do the owner *no good*'. He continues that 'the rogues of this world . . . know better; and, if the observation had been as true as it is old, would not have failed by this time to have discovered it'.

204

In for a penny, in for a pound. *If one has involved oneself in expense about a project one must go through with it even though the expense comes to much more than one intended.* The expression goes back two and a half centuries. **R.** in a play by Ravenscroft, 1695.

205

A Jack of all trades is master of none. *A person who follows many diverse occupations is never expert at any.* **R.** 1800, Maria Edgeworth.

The term 'Jack of all trades' goes back to early in the seventeenth century.

ABP : F   [69]

206

(1) Every Jack has (*or* must have) his Jill. (2) Jack shall have Jill. *Every man finds a mate.* The phrase 'Jacke shall have gyl' appears in Skelton early in the sixteenth century. 1611: A Jacke looks for a Gill. **R.** 1670, Ray.

207

Judge not, that ye be not judged. This is from *Matthew*, 7, 1, in the Sermon on the Mount. The passage continues: 'For with what judgment ye judge, ye shall be judged; and with what measure ye mete, it shall be measured to you again' (so in the Authorised Version; in the Revised Version, 'measured unto you').

208

Be just before you are generous. This comes in Sheridan's *School for Scandal* (IV, i) in 1777, but it appeared thirty years earlier in an essay by Mrs. Haywood.

209

The king can do no wrong. This is a maxim of the British constitution. 1689, Selden: The King can do no wrong, that is, no Process can be granted against him. 1765, Blackstone's *Commentaries*: The prerogative of the crown extends not to do any injury; it is created for the benefit of the people, and therefore cannot be exerted to their prejudice. The sentiment is legal, not moral.

210

Know thyself. Diogenes Laertius (A.D. 200–250) ascribes the origin of the injunction to the Greek philosopher Thales (seventh century B.C.). Juvenal says it came from heaven to an oracle. In English literature it is recorded first in 1531 in the writings of Sir Thomas Elyot: The words be these in Latine, *Nosce te ipsum*, whiche is in Englysshe, know thy selfe.

211

More know Tom Fool than Tom Fool knows. *We are known to more people than we know.* **A.** 1656: In all comedies more know the Clown than the Clown knows. **R.** 1723, Defoe.

212

You never know what you can do till you try. **R.** 1829, Marryat, *Frank Mildmay.*

213

Knowledge is power. **A.** *Proverbs*, 24, 5: A wise man is strong; yea, a man of knowledge increaseth strength. 1620, Bacon; *Ipsa scientia potestas est* [Knowledge itself is power], and *Scientia et potentia humana in idem coincidunt* [Knowledge and human power are synonymous].

214

He knows how many (blue) beans make five. *He is shrewd.* **R.** 1830, John Galt.

215

The labourer is worthy of his hire. *A person is entitled to a just remuneration for his work.* The phrase comes from *Luke*, 10, 7.

216

Lancashire thinks today what all England will think tomorrow. *O.D.E.P.* cites N. S. Lean in *Collectanea*, 1902–4, for the first record of the saying in print. A variation is: Manchester *thinks* today what London will *do* tomorrow.

217

The last straw breaks the camel's back. Figuratively, *a small thing, in itself apparently unimportant, but coming after many previous, weighty, troublesome things, is a culmination that is intolerable, and causes a breakdown or catastrophe.* **A.** 1645, Archbishop Bromhead: It is the last feather that breaks the horse's back. 1848, Dickens: As the last straw breaks the laden camel's back

218

Better late than never. Mr. Burton Stevenson quotes, as the first record of this thought, from the Greek of Dionysius of Halicarnassus (first century B.C.): It is better to be late than never to arrive. 1389, Chaucer, For bet than never is late. **R.** 1868 (title of farce).

219

It is too late to shut (*or* lock) the stable-door when the horse is stolen. Figuratively, *It is too late to take precautions against loss or damage when the mischief has been done.* In French, 1190, *A tart ferme on l'estable quant li chevaux est perduz* [Too late one shuts the stable when the horse has been stolen]. **R.** 1579, Pettie.

219a

Laugh, and the world laughs with you; Weep, and you weep alone. It is easier to gain agreement with, and a sharing of, your interests and feelings, in matters that cause you to be amused and cheerful, than to rouse sympathy in circumstances of sadness and sorrow, which you will be left to bear alone. The sentiment is expressed in a couplet by the American poetess, Ella Wheeler Wilcox (1855–1919).

It is expressed less cynically in *Romans* 12, 15: Rejoice with them that do rejoice and weep with them that weep.

220

He laughs best who laughs last. A. (1) 1591: Let them reioyce that at the ende doo win. (2) 1659: He laugheth that winneth. **R.** 1706, Vanbrugh, *The Country House.* 1823. Scott, *Peveril of the Peak*, quotes the French saying *Rira bien qui rira dernier.*

221

Hard cases make bad law. *Sound legislation is not based on exceptional cases.* **R.** in Lean's *Collectanea*, 1902–4.

222

A man may lead a horse to the water, but he cannot make it drink. *One may give a person good reasons, and provide him with opportunity or means, for doing a thing, but one cannot force him against his will to do it.* Heywood, 1546: A man maie well bring a horse to the water, but he cannot make him drink without he will. Dr. Johnson expanded the saying to 'but twenty cannot make him drink'.

223

A little learning is a dangerous thing. *A small amount of knowledge may mislead one and lead to wrong conclusions, principles, etc.* The words are a quotation from Pope's *Essay on Criticism*

> A little learning is a dang'rous thing;
> Drink deep, or taste not the Pierian spring;
> There shallow draughts intoxicate the brain.

[73]

'A little learning' is often misquoted as 'a little knowledge'.

224

Least said soonest (*or* is soonest) mended. There are, less common, variants, for **Least**, of **Little** or **Nothing**. *For healing a quarrel the best course is to stop discussing the matter.* **A.** 1460: Who sayth Lytell he is wyse, and fewe wordes are soone amended. 1555, Lyttle sayde, soone amended. **R.** 1818, Scott, *The Heart of Midlothian.*

225

Leave (*or* Let) well alone. *Do not change a state of things that is satisfactory lest you do harm.* **A.** 1386, Chaucer: Unwys is he that kan no wele endure.

Compare **Let sleeping dogs lie (94).**

226

Lend your money and lose your friend. *Lending money to a friend often leads to losing his friendship.* **A.** Hamlet (I, iii, 75)

> Neither a borrower nor a lender be,
> For loan oft loses both itself and friend.

Ray, 1670, has He that doth lend will lose his friend. He follows this with a translation of a French saying: He that lends to his friend loseth double, both money and friend. Seventy years later in Kelly the idea is found expressed in the form in which it has since remained current. Kelly adds: 'It is not the lending of our money that loses our friend, but the demanding it again'.

A recent variant is **If you lend a friend money you will lose either the money or the friend.**

[74]

227

The leopard cannot change its spots. Figuratively, *a person cannot change his inherited characteristics*. The expression is always applied derogatorily to qualities that are undesirable, 'spot' being used in a primary figurative sense of 'stain', 'blot', 'blemish'. The proverb is based on a passage in the Bible, *Jeremiah*, 13, 23: Can the Ethiopian change his skin, or the leopard his spots?

228

Liberty is not licence. 1645, Milton, *Sonnets*, vii: Licence they mean when they cry liberty. 1720, J. Sheffield: They are for licence, not for liberty.

229

There are lies, damned lies, and statistics. The meaning of this statement is that *statistics, unless handled with care by trained minds, often lead to seriously false conclusions*. Mr. Burton Stevenson quotes Mark Twain as in his autobiography attributing the remark to Disraeli, but adds that it has been attributed also to others.

230

Life is a pilgrimage. Life is described as a pilgrimage in the Bible (*Genesis*, 47, 9). Compare 1576, Pettie, 'the pilgrimage of this my short life'.

231

Life is sweet. A. 1350: Be monnes lode neuer so luther, the lyf is ay swete [However hard a man's load is, life is always sweet]. R. 1601.

[75]

232

Life is not all beer and skittles. *Life is not all pleasure, amusement, ease.* Dickens, *Pickwick Papers*: 'It's a regular holiday to them—all porter and skittles'. **R.** 1857, Hughes, *Tom Brown's Schooldays.*

233

Like to like (*or* **Like will to like**). *Things and people of the same sort are drawn to one another.* Cicero (106–43 B.C.) in *De Senectute* mentions the principle as proverbial. 1375, Lyk to lyk accordis wele.

234

One must draw the line somewhere. *There is a limit to what one will endure, or allow as right or permissible.* **A.** (in a passive form), 1878, Gilbert in *H.M.S. Pinafore*: The line must be drawn somewhere. **R.** 1887, Blackmore, *Springhaven.*

235

Listeners hear no good of themselves. 1647: The Old Proverb is, Hearkeners never heare good of themselves. **R.** 1678, Ray.

236

Little drops of water, little grains of sand, Make the mighty ocean and the pleasant land. Figuratively, *Minute and often apparently insignificant and negligible beginnings or efforts produce big and important results.* The lines are from a poem (1845) by Julia Carney (1823–1908).

237

Little (*or* **Small**) **pitchers have great** (*or* **long**, *or* **wide**) **ears.** Figuratively, *Children have sharp ears; so one should* *keep guard on saying things in their presence.* 'pitchers' = 'jugs'; 'ears' = their 'handles'. 1546, Heywood. The expression is a sort of pun on 'ear' (as 'handle' and 'human organ for hearing') and 'pitcher' (as 'jug' and 'human receptacle into which sound is poured').

238

Many a little makes a mickle. *Many little things or amounts accumulate to form a large thing or amount.* **A.** 1200: Thus ofte, ase me[n] seith, of lutel wacseth muchel [Thus oft, as men say, little waxeth (= increases) to much]. **R.** 1605, Camden. In the *Spectator*, 1712, the saying is as one of four maxims referring to the saving of money.

'mickle' is now obsolete except in this expression.

239

We live and learn. This phrase is used in two ways. (1) With **We**, or in the expression **One lives and learns,** it is a statement, mostly used as a reflection on an event that has greatly surprised us, and sometimes with a general implication that in our course through life many experiences are extremely strange. 1639, Clarke, who cites **We live and learn** as an English parallel of a Latin proverb by Erasmus that literally translated means 'We are made wiser by age'.

Less commonly it is used as an injunction, e.g. 1704, by Steele: Don't stand gaping, but live and learn, my lad.

240

Live and let live. *In living the sort of life that one chooses for oneself one should allow to others the right and means to do the same to suit their desires.* 1641, Ferguson's *Scottish Proverbs.* A writer on economics in the seventeenth century said that the proverb was an adaptation of a Dutch saying *Leuen ende laeien leuen.*

241

A living dog is better than a dead lion. *It is more desirable to be alive, even if one is an insignificant person, than to have been a great, important, person who is dead.* The statement comes from *Ecclesiastes*, 9, 4.

242

It is a long lane that has no turning. Figuratively, *misfortunes and troubles do not usually go on for ever.* The metaphor is that of a long lane, over difficult ground, that eventually has a turning leading into better conditions. 1670, Ray: It is a long run that never turns. **R.** 1748, Richardson, *Clarissa Harlowe*.

243

Look thy last on all things lovely every hour. This is a quotation from a poem by De la Mare (died 1958), 'Fare Well'. It continues

> Let no night
> Seal thy sense in deathly slumber
> Till to delight
> Thou hast paid thy utmost blessing.

244

Look before you leap. *Consider carefully possible difficulties and dangers before entering on a course. O.D.E.P.* cites as early as the fourteenth century in a German manuscript, with reference to thinking before speaking

> First loke and aftirward lepe;
> Avyse the well or [before] thow speke.

1528, Tyndale: Look ere thou leap. **R.** 1621, Burton's *Anatomy of Melancholy*.

Lookers-on see most of the game. Less common is **Lookers-on see more than players. A.** 1578: As at cheastes [chess], though skylfull players play, skyllesse [unskilled] vewers see, what they [the skylfull] omyt [fail to see]. The proverb is usually applied not to games and sports but figuratively to conduct, affairs, relations between people, etc. 1635, Howell: There is a true saying that the spectator oft-times sees more than the gamester. **R.** 1850, Smedley, *Frank Fairlegh*.

Love is blind. Chaucer, *The Marchantes Tale*: For love is blynd al day, and may nat see. *Two Gentlemen of Verona*: 'If you love her you cannot see her'; 'Why?' 'Because Love is blind.' Usually the blindness refers to the inability to see the defects in the loved one, but Shakespeare (who introduces the proverb into five plays) says in *The Merchant of Venice*

> But love is blind, and lovers cannot see
> The pretty follies that themselves commit.

The ancients sometimes represented Love (Greek, Eros; Latin, Cupid) with his eyes bandaged, so that he acts blindly.

Love laughs at locksmiths. A. *Venus and Adonis*

> Were beauty under twenty locks kept fast,
> Yet love breaks through and picks them all at
>   last.

In 1803 the words of the proverb were the title of a play by the younger Colman.

248

Love little and love long. This is an injunction against an immoderate love that does not last. 1546, Heywood: Old wise folk say 'Love me little, love me long'. *Romeo and Juliet*, I, vi, 14: Therefore love moderately; long love doth so.

249

Love is not love which alters when it alteration finds. This comes from Shakespeare's *Sonnets*, 116. It continues

> Or bends with the remover to remove:
> O, no! it is an ever-fixed mark,
> That looks on tempests and is never shaken . . .
> Love's not Time's fool, though rosy lips
>   and cheeks
> Within his bending sickle's compass come;
> Love alters not with his brief hours and weeks,
> But bears it out even to the edge of doom.
>   If this be error, and upon me prov'd,
>   I never writ, nor no man ever lov'd.

250

Love makes the world go round. Dante (Cary's translation): Love that moves the sun in heaven and all the stars. 1656, Cowley: 'Tis thou that mov'st the world through every part. R. 1865, Dickens, *Our Mutual Friend*.

251

Love me, love my dog. *If you love me, you must also love my dog.* This is often applied in a general sense with reference, apart from a dog, to loving a person's belongings, and to sharing his interests. In 1153 a sermon by St. Bernard has in Latin: *Qui me amat, amat et canem meum* [Who loves me loves also my dog]. 1480: He that lovythe me lovythe my hound.

The saying is one of the 'Popular Fallacies' of Lamb, who, however, after a description of being bitten by a friend's dog, digresses into an account of those other 'canine appendages . . . not always . . . in the shape of dogs', who to friendship add the intervention of some third anomaly, an impertinent dog, in the form of an uncongenial cousin, brother, uncle, son, acquaintance; or, if female, a tiger aunt or viper sister.

252

It is best to be off with the old love before you are on with the new. *O.D.E.P.* says the origin of this appears in a song in a play by R. Edwards, *Damon and Pythias* (1571): 'Tis good to be off wi' the old love before you are on wi' the new'. 1819, Scott, in *The Bride of Lammermoor*, mentioning it as 'an old song', has 'good' (instead of 'best' in the current version), and 'be on' (instead of 'are on').

253

The course of true love never did run smooth. *Midsummer Night's Dream*, I, i, 134.

254

Greater love hath no man than this (that a man should lay down his life for his friend). This is from *John*, 15, 13. In the original the last word is plural ('friends').

255

'Tis better to have loved and lost than never to have loved at all. This is from Section XXVII of Tennyson's *In Memoriam* (1850).

[81]

256

Lucky at cards, unlucky in love. The earliest recorded reference to this idea is in Swift (1738): 'Well, miss, you'll have a sad husband, you have such good luck at cards'. 1865, in a play by T. W. Robertson: 'I'm always lucky at cards'; 'Yes, I know an old proverb about that . . . Lucky at play, unlucky in ——'.

257

Every man is a fool or a physician at forty (*or thirty*). *By the time one reaches that age either one has learnt from experience how to keep oneself as healthy as possible, or one is a fool.* Professor W. S. Watt tells me that the thought contained in the proverb is adumbrated by two passages in Latin literature. Tacitus relates that the Emperor Tiberius used to mock at doctors and at those who after the age of thirty needed advice from them to know what benefited and harmed their constitution. Suetonius, again with reference to Tiberius, says that the emperor enjoyed excellent health although from the time he was thirty he looked after this according to his own judgment without the advice of doctors.

In English literature there are from the seventeenth century a number of references to men who are 'fools or physicians'. The first record of the proverb in its current form is in 1721, by Kelly.

258

The proper study of mankind is man. This is from Pope's *Essay on Man* (1733). Mr. Eric Partridge in his *Dictionary of Clichés* says that Pope took it from the French of Pierre Charron, 1541–1603.

Manners makyth (*or* **make**) **man** (*or* **the man**). A manuscript as early as the middle of the fourteenth century has: Maner makys man. There is ambiguity and variation about the precise meaning of 'manner' and 'manners' in early records. Kelly, 1721, in citing the proverb, uses 'manners' as a synonym of 'breeding'. In today's use it usually means 'morals', 'moral conduct'.

The proverb became commonly known as the motto of William of Wykeham, Bishop of Winchester, 1367–1404, founder of Winchester College and of New College, Oxford, which have adopted it as their motto.

Many heads are better than one. 1721, Kelly.

Compare **Four eyes see more than two** (122); and contrast **Too many cooks spoil the broth** (59).

So many men (*or* **heads**), **so many minds** (*or* **wits**). The earliest record of this thought is in Latin literature in a play by Terence: *Quot homines, tot sententiae* [As many men as they are, so many are their opinions]. Chaucer: As many hedes, as many wittes ther been. **R.** 1546, Heywood.

Marriage is a lottery. *It is chance whether one makes a happy or unhappy marriage.* There are adumbrations of this thought from the seventeenth century, but the first record of the current form is not until 1875, by Smiles, in *Thrift* (within inverted commas, as a proverb).

263

Marriages are made in heaven. 'made in heaven' = 'ordained by divine governance'. 1567, W. Painter: True it is that marriage be don in heaven and performed on earth. **R.** 1580, Lyly.

264

A young man married is a young man marred. This is from *All's Well that Ends Well*, II, iii. The words in the original are 'a man that's marr'd'. Kipling has

> You may carve it on his tombstone, you may write
>   it on his card,
> A young man married is a young man marred.

We may contrast this with the preceding proverb, and compare it with the following one. It is one of the many proverbs where a general statement may well have particular exceptions.

265

Marry in haste, and repent at leisure. A. (1) 1546, Heywood: It is true thys proverbe olde, Hastie love is soone hot and colde. And once their heat a little controlde, Then perceive they well, hot love soon colde. (2) 1566, W. Painter: . . . leaste, in making haste choise, leasure for repentaunce shuld folow. *III Henry VI*, IV, i, 18: Hasty marriage seldom proveth well. 1614, J. Day in a sermon uses the expression 'marrying in haste and repenting at leisure'. **R.** 1670, Ray.

266

Like master like man. *The servant takes after his master.* The idea is of great antiquity, and there are equivalent sayings in French, German, Italian, Spanish. It is found in the Bible in *Isaiah* (24, 2), 'as with the servant, so with the master'. Erasmus in his *Adagia* quotes Cicero saying in a letter *Qualis hera, talis pedisequae* [As the mistress is, so are her waiting women]. A century later another Latin writer says *Qualis dominus, talis servus* [As the master is, so is his slave]. Udall in 1548, translating Erasmus, writes: Beeying lyke men lyke maister according to the proverbe. **R.** 1568, Fulwell.

267

A man cannot serve two masters. Figuratively, *a person cannot satisfactorily devote himself to two different causes that have different and opposed aims.* The origin of the proverb is in the Bible: *Matthew*, 6, 24, and *Luke*, 16, 13, where the injunction is followed by 'Ye cannot serve God and mammon'.

268

Maxima debetur puero reverentia. This comes from Satire XIV of the Roman poet Juvenal (born in the first century A.D.; the precise dates of his life are not known). Literally it says *The greatest reverence is due to a boy.* It is generally used with a rather more general application, meaning that *great respect is due to boys and girls, on account of their innocence and especially of the responsibility their innocent shoulders bear for the future.*

269

There is a mean (*or* measure) in all things. *Nothing should be done or felt in excess.* The thought, which is very old and widespread, is found in Greek and Sanskrit five centuries B.C. **A.** Chaucer: In every thyng, I woot, there lith [lieth] measure. **R.** 1509.

270

One man's meat is another man's poison. *What is liked by or beneficial to one person is disliked by or harmful to another.*

ABP : G   [85]

Lucretius wrote *Quod cibus est alii, aliis fuat acre venenum* [What is food to one man may be bitter poison to others]. In English literature **R.** 1614.

271

Every medal has its reverse. Figuratively, *in every situation or set of circumstances there is a second, alternative, different, contrary, aspect, interpretation, explanation.* We use the word 'side' in a similar sense, as for example, 'There is another side to that question'. The earliest date of a recorded use of the proverb is 1603, in Florio's translation of Montaigne, who mentions an Italian form of the statement. 1842, Lever: Happily there is a reverse to the medal.

272

Memento mori. (Latin) *Remember you must die.* I have been unable to trace this in Latin literature or to find an early date for its record in English literature. Mr. Burton Stevenson, referring to it as 'the motto of the Order of the Death's Head', quotes from the Latin poet Persius (A.D. 34–62), *Satires*, V, 153: *Vive memor leti, fugit hora* [Live mindful of death; the hour flies].

273

The quality of mercy is not strained. ('strained' = 'constrained' or 'forced'). *One must not be stingy, sparing, mean, in the degree or kind of compassion, kindness, clemency, one gives.* The expression comes from *The Merchant of Venice*, IV, i, where Portia is pleading with Shylock.

274

De minimis curat non lex. This is a Latin legal apothegm, *The law does not trouble to concern itself in minute matters.*

It is often used popularly, apart from legal matters, in discussion etc., to mean that *the given point is too trivial, unimportant, negligible, to be taken into consideration.*

275

Misery (*or* Adversity) makes (*or* acquaints men with) strange bedfellows. In modern uses of this proverb 'bed-fellows' means associates and companions with whom one is brought into close and familiar relations. R. *The Tempest*, II, ii. In 1849 Bulwer Lytton for **misery** or **adversity** substituted **poverty.**

276

Misfortunes (*or* Troubles) seldom (*or* never) come singly (*or* alone). A. 1300, *King Alisaunder*: Men telleth, in olde mone [remembrance], The qued [harm] commth nowher alone. *Hamlet*, IV, 5: When sorrows come, they come not single spies, But in battalions. *O.D.E.P.* gives a number of records from the fourteenth to the seventeenth centuries with variants, for 'Misfortunes' or 'Troubles', of 'Hardship', 'Sorrow', 'Evil', 'Mishap', 'Loss', 'Woe'. R. 1682, in a translation from German.
Compare **It never rains but it pours (354).**

277

The (*or* Our) worst misfortunes are those that never happen (*or* befall us). *The troubles from which we suffer most are those that in our anxious imaginings we fear and worry about, but that never do happen.* Mr. Burton Stevenson cites J. R. Lowell as using the expression in 1884. In the following year E. P. Hood includes it in a book of proverbs, mentioning, as an illustration of its meaning, a couplet by Emerson (who died in 1882):

What torments of pain you endured
From the griefs that never arrived.

[87]

278

He who makes no mistakes makes nothing. *The person who makes no mistakes never does anything of value.* 1868, Bishop Magee: The man who makes no mistakes does not usually make anything.

279

A miss is as good as a mile. *Failure by however little is still failure (S.O.E.D.).* *To miss doing or getting a thing by even the smallest distance or amount is as serious, disastrous, fatal, as by a great distance or amount.* The phrasing of the idiom is loose. It is not a 'miss' that is comparable with a 'mile'; but some distance or amount, however small, e.g. an inch or a second. Moreover the 'miss' is not as 'good' as a 'mile', but as 'bad'. The date of the earliest record of the proverb in this form is 1825, by Scott. There was formerly a proverb, **An inch in a miss is as good as an ell.**

280

Money begets (*or* breeds, *or* gets, *or* makes) money. 1572, Wilson, *Discourses upon Usury*: Money getteth money. 1593, Shakespeare, *Venus and Adonis*: Gold that's put to use more gold begets. 1678, Ray ('begets'). 1776, Adam Smith ('makes'). 1841, Marryat, *The Poacher* ('breeds').

281

The love of money is the root of all evil. This saying comes from *I Timothy*, 6, 10. A Greek epigram, which Mr. Burton Stevenson translates as 'The love of money is the mother-city of all evils', is ascribed to the cynic philosopher Diogenes (fourth century B.C.).

Mark Twain (perhaps jocularly) and Bernard Shaw (probably seriously) said: 'Poverty is the root of all evils'.

[88]

The use of the word 'all' in these sayings is a manifest exaggeration.

282

Money is a good servant but a bad master. 1633, Massinger, *A New Way to Pay Old Debts*. The same statement is applied to fire and to water; e.g. 1733, Swift: Why, fire and water are good servants, but they are bad masters.

283

Money is the sinews of war. Money is essential for waging war successfully in the way that sinews are needed in the body to connect muscles with bones, etc., and make movement possible. The phrase has been adopted from one used by Cicero: *nervos belli pecuniam infinitam* [sinews of war, infinite treasure]. *O.D.E.P.* cites Bacon as having said in parliament in 1592: Laws are the sinews of peace, money of war; but to some extent he contradicts this in his *Essays* (1525) by saying: Neither is money the Sinewes of Warre (as it is trivially said) where the Sinewes of Men's Armes, in Base and Effeminate People, are failing.

1732, Fuller: Money is the sinew of love as well as of war.

284

De mortuis nil nisi bonum. (Latin) *Of the dead say nothing but what is good;* or in another interpretation, *If one cannot speak well of the dead, keep silent about them.* Diogenes Laertius (A.D. 200–50), who wrote in Greek, says: Speak no evil of the dead; but Mr. Burton Stevenson points out that Plutarch quotes the statement as originating more than three centuries earlier in Solon's Laws. The injunction is generally used with reference to those who have died lately.

285

If the mountain will not come to Mahomet, Mahomet must go to the mountain. This is generally used in a loose way to mean that, *if things do not happen in the easy and convenient way one wants or hopes, one must make the best of matters, put aside pride, and go out of one's way by effort and sacrifice to gain one's object;* or that, *if a person will not do a thing in the way he wants, he must do it, or get it done, in the only way he can.*

Bacon's *Essays* (1625): 'Mahomet made the people believe that he would call an hill to him and from the top of it offer up his prayer. Mahomet called the hill to come to him again and again; and when the hill stood still, he was never a whit abashed, but said "If the hill will not come to Mahomet, Mahomet will go to the hill"'.

286

Murder will out. A. 1300: For-thi sais into this tyde, Is no man that murther may hide [Therefore as we say today, there is no man who can hide murder]. *O.D.E.P.* and Apperson cite many records of the sentiment from Chaucer to Shakespeare and to modern times. It expresses a comfortable doctrine, but many murders and many murderers are never discovered.

287

Music has charms. This comes from the opening words in Congreve's *Mourning Bride* (1697)

> Music hath charms to soothe a savage breast,
>   To soften rocks, or bend a knotted oak.

288

(1) What is, must be. (2) What has been, had to be. These dicta express the principles of the philosophical doctrine of

Determinism (as opposed to the belief in Free Will), that *everything, physical, mental, spiritual, is the inevitable result of a previous inevitable cause that in its turn was an inevitable result.* Compare Marlowe, *Doctor.Faustus* (*c.* 1590)

> What doctrine call you this, *Che sara, sara*?
> What will be, shall be.

translating an old Italian proverb, which must have been known to Chaucer also.

289

What must be, must be. It is strange if this truism is not old, but the earliest date for its record given by *O.D.E.P.* does not go further back than the middle of the nineteenth century.

290

Nature abhors a vacuum. Plutarch (A.D. 46–120) in *Moralia* says (Holland's translation, 1603): There is no voidness or vacuity in nature. 1642, Fuller (the divine): Queen Joan (hating widowhood as much as nature doth vacuum) married James, King of Majorca. The earliest record of the current English form of the statement is in Boswell's *Life*, where Dr. Johnson, applying the principle to man's mind, says 'Whatever philosophy may determine of material nature, it is certainly true of intellectual nature, that it *abhors a vacuum*; our minds cannot be empty'.

291

Nature will have its course. 1400: For kynde [nature] will have his course. R. 1580, Lyly: Nature will have hir cause.

292

One touch of nature makes the whole world kin. This comes from Shakespeare's *Troilus and Cressida*, III, iii, 175.

The argument is rather complicated. In common usage the statement is generally used to mean that the manifestation of a fundamental emotion in human nature brings everyone together in sympathetic concord.

293

Though you cast out nature with a fork, it will still return. *One cannot by force banish natural characteristics.* This is a translation of the words of Horace (65–68 B.C.) in one of his odes: *Naturam expelles furca, tamen usque recurret* [You may expel nature with a pitchfork; nevertheless it will come back]. 1539, Taverner: Thrust out nature with a croche, yet wyll she styll runne backe agayne. ('croche' = 'crook'. a hook or shepherd's staff).

Compare **What is bred in the bone will not out of the flesh** (30).

294

The nearer the bone, the sweeter the flesh. 1559: The nigher the bone, the flesh is much sweeter. **R.** 1639.

Kelly, 1721, gives **Flesh is aye fairest that is farthest from the bone,** adding 'Spoken to them who are plump and look well'.

295

Necessity is the mother of invention. There are various adumbrations, from early in the sixteenth century, extolling necessity as the teacher of wit, the inventor of good things, the mother of productions, the maker of craftsmen; but the earliest recorded date of its being called the 'mother of invention' is 1726, by Swift.

296

Necessity has (*or* knows) no law. The ancient Greek poet Simonides says that even the gods war not with necessity;

and Plutarch that God yields to necessity. The Romans had a legal maxim of which our current saying is the exact equivalent: *Necessitas non habet legem*. In English literature the earliest records, from the fourteenth century, have, not 'necessity', but 'need'; in 1555, however, 'Necessitie hath no law' is referred to as as a 'common saying'.

This cynical statement may be compared with **All is fair in love and war** (127) for its lack of high morality.

297

Needles and pins, needles and pins:
When a man marries his trouble begins.
This comes from a collection of nursery rhymes published in 1843, and may be compared with Nos. 194, 264–265.

298

Needs must when the devil drives. *One must submit to hard necessity.* 'Needs' here is an Old English adverb, meaning 'necessarily', 'of necessity', almost obsolete except when used here with 'must'. The 'devil' is taken as a symbol of an unpleasantly powerful force whipping on a team of horses. 1420, Lydgate: For hit ys oft seyde by hem that yet lyues [who has kept his life (by doing this)] 'He must nedys go that the deuell dryues'. Records from the fifteenth to the early nineteenth centuries have 'needs go', including *All's Well That Ends Well* (I, iii); later 'go' was dropped.

299

It is a foolish (*or* foul, *or* ill) bird that defiles (*or* fouls) its own nest. *It is a foolish person who speaks ill of his own family or other connections.* 1250, *Owl and Nightingale*: Dahet habbe that ilke best That fuleth his owe nest [A curse be upon that beast that defiles his own nest]. 1402, Hoccleve: An olde proverbe seyde ys in englyssh: men seyn 'that brid or foule ys dyshonest, what that he be and holden ful

[93]

chirlyssh, that vseth to defoule his oone neste'. Throughout the centuries there was a number of variants from the verbs and adjectives given in the heading.

300

He who handles a nettle tenderly is soonest stung. Figuratively, *when one is dealing with troublesome people and affairs, the use of gentle methods will subject one to harsh and painful reaction, from which you will not suffer if you employ drastic measures.* 1579, Lyly: True it is that hee which toucheth the nettle tenderly is soonest stoung. 1753, Aaron Hill, 'The Nettle's Lesson'

> Tender-handed stroke a nettle
> And it stings you for your pains;
> Grasp it like a man of mettle,
> And it soft as silk remains.

301

Never do things by halves. The thought is in *Ecclesiastes*, 9, 10: Whatsoever thy hand findeth to do, do it with thy might. 1733, Hanway: He never did things by halves. **R.** 1883, Charles Reade.

302

Never too late to mend. 1655, Howell: It is never over late to mend. **R.** 1856, in title of Charles Reade's novel.

303

Never is a long day. A. Chaucer: Nevere to thryve were to [too] long a date. 1721, Kelly: Never is a long term. **R.** 1839, Dickens, *Nicholas Nickleby*.

304

Never too old (*or* late) to learn. The Romans had a proverb that one must go on learning as long as one lived. In English literature, Thomas Middleton, 1627: A man is never too old to learn.

305

Never say die. *Never give in; Never abandon hope.* **R.** 1837, Dickens, *Pickwick Papers*.

306

Never the time and the place and the loved one all together. This is from Browning's poem, 'Never the time and the place' (1883).

307

A new broom sweeps clean. Figuratively, *People newly appointed to posts make drastic changes.* 1546, Heywood: The greene new brome sweepth cleene. (Fresh green twigs would be more pliable than those that were dry.) **R.** 1579.

308

Ill news travels (*or* flies, *or* comes) fast (*or* apace). A. 1603, Drayton: Ill news hath wings, and with the wind doth go. 1671, Milton: Evil news rides post, while good news baits. **R.** 1678, Ray.

309

There is nothing new under the sun. *Ecclesiastes*, 1, 9: There is no new thing under the sun. Bernard Shaw, 1903, turned 'no thing' into 'nothing'.

310

No news is good news. *When there is bad news to fear, it is comforting to reflect that to receive none means almost certainly there is none that is bad and probably some that is good.* The proverb was partly anticipated four centuries ago in the *Loseley MSS.*: No newis is better than evill newis. 1632, D. Lupton: The best news is when we have no news.

311

Noblesse oblige. (French) In literal translation, *Noble birth compels; i.e. to be of noble birth imposes, carries with it, entails, responsibility and obligations.* The thought is as old as Æschylus.

312

Nothing is so bad but it might have been worse. (A reflection with which to console oneself, in thought or word, when things are in a bad way, to prevent one from becoming utterly desperate.) 1876, Mrs. Bank, *A Manchester Man*: There is nothing so bad but it might be worse.

313

Nothing comes from (*or* out of) nothing. The thought is common in antiquity. It first appears in the Greek poet Alcaeus (sixth to seventh century B.C.). In the philosophy of Epicurus (third to fourth century B.C.) it is the principle that serves as the foundation of the whole physical theory. It is enunciated by Lucretius (first century B.C.) in *De Rerum Natura*. In the first century A.D. it is ridiculed by the Roman satirist Persius.

The Latin form of the proverb was *Nihil ex nihilo fit.* The words of Boethius (A.D. 564) are *Nihil ex nihilo existere vera sententia est* [It is a true opinion that nothing comes into existence out of nothing]. Chaucer translates this in *Boethius*: For this sentence is verray and soth that 'nothing ne hath his beynge of naught'. 1592, Marlowe: Of naught is nothing made. *King Lear*, I, i, 90: Nothing will come of nothing.

314

Nothing venture, nothing have. A. Chaucer: He which that no-thing under-taketh, No-thing ne acheveth. 1546, Heywood: Nought venter nought have. **R.** 1602.

315

The offender never pardons. 1640, Herbert. Today the thought is probably more often expressed in Dryden's lines (1672): Forgiveness to the injur'd does belong, But they ne'er pardon who have done the wrong.

316

The old order changeth. This phrase, often quoted with the words that follow, **yielding place to new,** comes from *Morte d'Arthur*, which Tennyson (1809–92) used again in the revised poem, *The Passing of Arthur*.

317

A man is as old as he feels, and a woman as old as she looks. 1855, Mortimer Collins (with 'as he's feeling').

318

Omelets are not made without breaking (*or* **breaking of) eggs.** *There are some things that cannot be done without drastic or violent action, or sacrificing something.* The proverb appears first in French, *On ne peut pas faire des omelettes sans casser des oeufs*, recorded of Robespierre, and as a remark by a French person in Haydon's *Autobiography*

(1815). In an English form the first recorded use of the metaphor is in 1859. **R.** 1898 in *The Times*.

319

One man may steal a horse while another may not look over the hedge. Figuratively, *One man is allowed, or manages, to commit a big iniquity without being punished, whereas another is brought to book for a trivial offence.* 1546, Heywood: This prouerbe . . . that some man maie steale a hors better Than some other may stande and looke vpone. 1591, Lyly: Some men may better steale a horse then another looke ouer the hedge.

320

One swallow does not make a summer. Figuratively, *A single incident, act, example, etc., does not provide the required condition for establishing a principle, etc.* The English proverb is adapted from the Greek of Aristotle's *Ethics*, which says that one swallow does not make spring. In Erasmus's *Adagia*, 1500, this appears in a Latin form. Taverner in his edition of the *Adagia* (1539) substitutes 'summer' for 'spring': It is not one swallow that bryngeth in somer; and he adds a human application, It is not one good qualitie that meketh a man good.

321

He who pays the piper can call the tune. Literally, *He who pays the player can decide what tune shall be played.* Figuratively, *He who bears the cost, stands the expense, has the right to decide what shall be done.* The 'piper' was one who played on a pipe, especially a strolling musician; and in Scotland he is a 'bag-piper'. I have not found an early appearance of the proverb, or heard of adumbrations earlier than in the *Daily News* in 1895, and the *Spectator* in 1910.

The original and different idea of the statement was that, if one wanted to dance, one must pay the piper or fiddler. 1638, J. Taylor: Alwayes those that dance must pay the musike..

322

If you want peace, be prepared for war. This is usually expressed in the Latin phrase *Si vis pacem, para bellum* [If you want peace, prepare for war], an adaptation of Vegetius's words, *Qui desiderat pacem preparet bellum* [Let him who desires peace prepare for war]. The earliest date of a recorded use of the maxim in an English form is 1885.

323

Take care of the pence, and the pounds will take care of themselves. 1750, Lord Chesterfield, in a letter, wrote that this used to be said by the Secretary of the Treasury.

324

A penny saved is a penny gained. *Money that, instead of being spent, has been kept, one can count equivalent to that amount earned.* **A.** 1640, Herbert: A penny spared is twice got. **R.** 1662, Fuller (the divine).

325

He who touches pitch will be defiled. *Apocrypha, Ecclesiasticus*, 13, 1: He that toucheth pitch shall be defiled therewith. 1303, Manning: Who so handlyth pycche wellyng [boiling] hote, He shal haue fylthe thereof sumdeyl [in some degree]. The expression is used figuratively in *I Henry IV* (II, iv).

326

Pity is akin to love. A. *Twelfth Night* (III, i): 'I pity you.' 'That's a degree to love.' **R.** 1696.

327

There is a place for everything, and everything in its place. 1875, Smiles, *Thrift*.

328

One cannot be in two places at once. A. 1655, Gurnall ('One cannot be found . . .'). 1842, W. H. Maxwell ('Nothing can be . . .').

329

A poet is born, not made. This is a translation of the Latin maxim *Poeta nascitur, non fit.* 1581, Sidney: Therefore is it an old prouerbe, *Orator fit; poeta nascitur* [An orator becomes one; a poet is born so]. 1620, Shelton: A poet is naturally born a poet from his mother's womb. 1662, Fuller (the divine): One is not made but born a poet.

330

Politeness (*or* Civility) costs nothing, *or* One never loses anything by politeness. The statements are usually made where with reference to a particular situation or circumstances a person deplores that politeness had not been shown, and suggests or implies that it ought to be or to have been. 1762, Lady Mary Wortley Montagu: Politeness costs nothing and gains everything.

331

Any port in a storm. Figuratively, *in extreme difficulties or dangers one welcomes any escape, relief, help.* **R.** 1780, Cobb, *The First Floor*.

Poverty is no sin. No-one today would consider it necessary to say or write this, but that was not always so. Herbert in 1640 has it in his book of proverbs, and at the same period Henry Peacham (painter, musician, mathematician, expert in heraldry, epigrammatist) wrote, as if he was enunciating a strange and remarkable truth: 'Women of the meanest condition make good wives'.

When poverty comes in at the door, love flies (*or* **goes,** *or* **jumps,** *or* **leaps**) **out of** (*or* **at**) **the window.** *Poverty is destructive of love in married life.* **A.** (1) 1631, Brathwait: It hath been an old maxime that, as poverty goes in at one door, love goes out at the other. (2) 1639, Clarke, When povertie comes in at doores, love leapes out at windowes. 1732, Fuller, 'creeps out'; 'door' is perhaps used as a symbol of the channel of practical troubles; 'window', of love's sunshine. **R.** 1823, Galt.

In a more general way than to love the sentiment has in the past been applied to friendship and companionship. It is found in the ancient classical writers in Menander: (translation) When a man is faring badly friends clear out of the way. In 1659 Clarke, in addition to the quotation given above in 1639, has When good cheare is lacking Our friends will go packing; and in Kelly (1721) it is friendship that 'flees out at the window'. Kelly gives also in Latin *Cum fortuna perit, nullus amicus* [When prosperity perishes, there will be no friend].

The earliest record in English literature bearing on poverty as a destroyer of friendship is in 1350 in the *Douce MS.*: Poverte brekys company. Chaucer has And if thy fortune change that thou wexe poore, farewell friendshipe and felowshipe. Hoccleve (1405) writes in the same strain, followed by others from the sixteenth to the eighteenth

ABP : H [101]

century. *O.D.E.P.* and Apperson record as established proverbs on this theme, from Heywood, 1546: pouertie parteth felowship (*or* friends, *or* good company), and from Howell, 1659: In times of prosperity friends will be plenty; In times of adversity not one among twenty, and Fuller, 1732 etc.

334

Practice makes perfect. This maxim is the same as the Romans had, *Usus promptum facit.* The collocation of 'practice' and 'perfect' is recorded first in 1560. 1564, Bullein: Use maketh perfectness. **R.** 1810, Crabbe.

335

Practise what you preach. A. (1) 1377, Langland: If ye lyven as ye leren us, we shal leve yow the bettere [If you live as you teach us, we shall believe you more readily]. (2) *The Merchant of Venice* (I, ii, 15): It is a good divine that follows his own instructions. **R.** 1812, Combe, *Dr. Syntax*: You should practise what you preach.

336

Put your trust in God, but keep your powder dry. *Have faith that God will order things for the best, but do not neglect practical precautions.* Keeping the powder dry is an allusion to the time when soldiers carried on them the gunpowder for their muskets. The injunction was uttered by Cromwell, who, when his soldiers were about to cross a river, ended his address to them with the exhortation 'Put your trust in God, but mind to keep your powder dry'. There is an Arab proverb, **Put your trust in God, but tie up the leg of your camel,** based on a statement by Mahomet: 'Hobbling, put your trust in God'.

There is no time like the present (that is to say, for doing something that has to be done). 1771, Smollett, *Humphrey Clinker*. Compare **Procrastination is the thief of time (341), Never put off till tomorrow what can be done today (348). Take time by the forelock (415).**

Prevention is better than cure. A. 1630: Prevention is so much better than healing. 1685: The wisdom of prevention is better than the wisdom of remedy. 1732, Fuller: Prevention is much preferable to Cure. **R.** 1850, Dickens, *Martin Chuzzlewit*.

Every man has his price. This 'shallow maxim of worldly cynicism', as Liddon described it, is often thought to have been uttered first by Sir Robert Walpole (1676–1745). Horace Walpole (1717–95) denied that the statement was made by his father, to whom, he claimed, it was attributed by his enemies. Sir William Wyndham, who was partly contemporary with Sir Robert Walpole, wrote in *The Bee* (1734): 'It is an old maxim that every man has his price.' The idea is at least as old as Epictetus (first century A.D.). One may perhaps say that 'thousands of exceptions prove the rule'. (See 115.)

Pride will have (*or* comes before) a fall. A. *Proverbs*, 16, 18: Pride goeth before destruction, and an haughty spirit before a fall. 1390, Gower: Pride . . . which God himself hath in desdeign, that, thogh it mount for a throwe, it schal doun fall and overthrowe [Pride . . . which God himself despises, so that, although it rises up for a short time, it

[103]

will fall down and be overthrown]. 1509, Barclay: Foule pryde wyll have a fall. **R.** 1546, Heywood.

341

Procrastination is the thief of time. 1742, Young's *Night Thoughts*. Compare **There is no time like the present (337), Never put off till tomorrow what can be done today (348), Take time by the forelock (415).**

342

The proof of the pudding is in the eating. Figuratively, *it is only experience of the results that will show the value of some arrangement, plan, theory, etc., in the same way that only the eating and tasting of a pudding proves how good the ingredients were and how skilful the cooking has been.* **A.** 1300: Hit is y-written, every thing Himself sheweth in tasyting. 1623, Camden: All the proofe of a pudding is in the eating. **R.** 1714, Addison.

343

It is easy to prophesy after the event. *After an event has happened, it is easy to say one knew it would happen.*
I have not been able to find when this expression first came into use.
Compare **It is easy to be wise after the event (446).**

344

A prophet is not without honour save in his own country. *It is in one's ordinary surroundings, among one's close acquaintances, friends, countrymen, that one is refused the recognition, respect, honour, that one is given elsewhere.* The saying comes from *Matthew*, 13, 57.

Man proposes (*or* **and,** *or* **but**) **God disposes.** *Human beings make plans; God settles things in a different way.* Compare *Proverbs*, 16, 9: A man's heart deviseth his way: but the Lord directeth his steps. In a translation of the Latin of Thomas à Kempis's *De Imitatione Christi*, 1450: Man purposith and God disposith. **R:** 1853.

Providence is always on the side of the strongest battalions. *Victory and success always come to those who are the strongest and most powerful.* This statement is adapted from a sentence in a letter by Voltaire (1770): *On dit que Dieu est toujours pour les gros bataillons* [It is said that God is always on the side of the big battalions]. In English the sentiment is recorded as expressed first in 1842 by Alison in his *History of Europe*: Moreau expressed a fact of general application, explained according to the irreligious ideas of the French Revolution, when he said that 'Providence was always on the side of the dense battalions'.

One cannot put back the clock. *One cannot change circumstances and conditions that have occurred, developed, evolved, or restore them to the state in which they were before.* **A.** 1907, A. C. Benson, *Upton Letters*. G. K. Chesterton (1874–1936) in one of his essays, dealing with the statement, says that the clock can be put back because it was made by man, and what man has done he can undo.

Never put off till tomorrow what can be done (*or* **you can do**) **today.** **A.** Chaucer: An old proverb seith that the goodnesse that thou mayst do this day, do it, and abyde nat ne delaye it nat till tomorwe. 1616, Draxe: Deferre not vntill to morrow, if thou canst do it to day. **R.** 1749, Chesterfield, *Letters*. Compare **There is no time like the present (337)**, **Procrastination is the thief of time (341)**, **Take time by the forelock (415)**.

349

It takes two to make a quarrel. 1732, Fuller, *Gnomologia*: There must be two at least to a quarrel.

R. 1859, Henry Kingsley, *Geoffrey Hamlyn*. The idea is as old as Socrates.

350

Quem (*or* Quos) Deus vult perdere, prius dementat. *Whom God would ruin he first sends mad.* There are expressions of this thought in Greek and Latin literature. In English literature it is recorded first in 1640, by Herbert: Whom God will punish, he will first take away the understanding. 1687, Dryden:

> For those whom God to ruine has design'd
> He fits for Fate, and first destroys their Mind.

351

Ask no questions and you will be told no lies. **A.** 1773, Goldsmith, *She Stoops to Conquer*: Ask me no questions and I'll tell you no fibs. **R.** 1860, Dickens, *Great Expectations*: Drat that boy. Ask no questions and you'll be told no lies.

352

The race is not to the swift, nor the battle to the strong. This quotation from *Ecclesiastes*, 9, 11, is generally used to mean that, as Burton expresses it in the *Anatomy of Melan-*

choly (1621), the fortunes of men are advanced 'not by honesty, learning, worth, wisdom', but by 'chance', and by what he calls 'time', presumably meaning 'occasion'.

353

Rain before seven: fine (*or* shine) before eleven. The only record of this by *O.D.E.P.* is in a letter in *Notes and Queries* in 1853. There is a proverbial variation: *If it rains at eleven, 'twill last till seven.*

354

It never (*or* seldom) rains but it pours. *Troubles never come singly.* '*It cannot rain but it pours*' is the title of a book by J. Arbuthnot in 1726. A year later 'It never rains but it pours' is the title of an essay by Swift in the first volume of a *Supplement to Dr. Swift's and Mr. Pope's Works* (which contains also work by Arbuthnot and Gay).

Compare **Misfortunes (*or* Troubles) (seldom *or* never) come singly (*or* alone)** in 276.

355

Rats leave (*or* desert, *or* forsake) a sinking ship (*or* falling house). The statement is generally used today with reference to human beings who leave an occupation or desert a cause when they foresee its decline or failure.

The Elder Pliny (A.D. 23–79) in his *Natural History* says that, before a house falls, mice leave it. In English literature in 1601 Holland's translation of Pliny mentions this. Shakespeare in *The Tempest* describes rats as instinctively quitting a sinking ship. Bacon in *Essays* (1597) reverts from 'ship' to 'house'. Applied in a general sense to human affairs the metaphor is first recorded as used in 1824 by Scott in *St. Ronan's Well*.

356

Reading makes a full man, conference a ready man, writing an exact man. This is a quotation from Bacon's *Essays* (1597).

Benjamin Franklin (1738) wrote: Reading makes a full man—meditation a profound man—discourse a clear man.

357

Red sky in the morning is shepherd's (*or* sailor's) warning: red sky at night is shepherd's (*or* sailor's) delight. This belief is referred to by Christ (*Matthew*, 16, 2 and 3). *O.D.E.P.* gives three references to it in the sixteenth century, including Shakespeare's in *Venus and Adonis*. There is then no record of it until the current form near the end of the nineteenth century.

The same expression of warning or delight has been applied to a rainbow.

358

Always verify your references. *Confirm the correctness of quotations you have cited. O.D.E.P.* assigns the origin of this dictum to M. J. Routh (1755–1854, President of Magdalen College, Oxford).

359

Render unto Caesar the things that are Caesar's and unto God the things that are God's. This is from *Matthew*, 22, 21. *Do your duty as a citizen to the State, and obey the law; but do not let those practices be confused or interfere with your religious and moral duties.*

360

Revenge is sweet. 1566, N. Painter: Vengeance is sweete. 1609, Ben Jonson: O revenge, how sweet art thou. 1667,

Milton, *Paradise Lost*, IX, evenge, 11: R at first, though sweet, Bitter ere long, back on itself recoils. **R.** 1775, Sheridan, *St. Patrick's Day*. The proverb seems to be a direct contradiction to the biblical "Vengeance is mine . . . saith the Lord', *Romans* 12, 9.

361

A rolling stone gathers no moss. Figuratively, *a person who is constantly moving and changing from one place or occupation to another will never gain a steady, established, position.* There was an ancient Greek maxim about this that Erasmus cited in *Adagia* (1550) and translated into Latin. Two centuries earlier Langland has: Syldon mossyth the Marbelston that men ofte treden. **R.** 1546, Heywood.

Contrast *Two Gentlemen of Verona*, I, i, 2: Home-keeping youth have ever homely wits.

362

Rome was not built in a day. Figuratively, *Great and important things cannot be accomplished in a short time.* The proverb is found in French as early as the twelfth century. In English literature, 1539, Taverner.

363

When you are at Rome do as the Romans do (*or* as Rome does). *Adapt your conduct to that of those in whose company you are.* Jeremy Taylor cites this injunction, in Latin, with a translation, from a letter by St. Augustine, in the fourth century, as advice given by St. Ambrose. 1530, R. Hill, *Commonplace Book*: Whan thou art at Rome, do after the dome; And whan thou art els where, do as they do ther. 1669, Penn: 'When thou art at Rome, thou must do as Rome does'.

364

There is no rose without a thorn. Lydgate (1370–1451): There is no rose in garden but there be sum thorne. **R.** 1670, Ray. From the seventeenth century onwards the expression is generally used figuratively: e.g. *I Henry VI*, II, iv, 69.

Horticulturally there is an exception to the rule in the rose Zephyrine Drouhin, the Thornless Rose.

365

There is no royal road to learning. This was said over two thousand years ago, about geometry, by Euclid, the Greek mathematician, to Ptolemy I, King of Egypt. In English literature the first record of the statement is in 1857, by Trollope, in *Barchester Towers*.

366

It is better to be safe than sorry. *It is better to take a course that leaves you safe, sound, and at ease, than a venturesome and risky one that may lead to disaster and regrets.* This is one of the few proverbs that have been added to our language in recent years, and may be a development of the slogan **Safety First**, which appeared first in the report of the Council of Industrial Safety in 1915.

367

It will be all the same (*or* one) a hundred (*or* thousand) years hence. A. 1611: All will be one at the latter day. 1738, Swift: My comfort is, 'twill be all one a thousand years hence. 1839, Dickens, *Nicholas Nickleby*, Mrs. Squeers frequently remarked when she made any mistake, it would be all the same a hundred years hence.

What is sauce for the goose is sauce for the gander. *What applies to one person applies equally to another.* The allusion is to sauce that is equally palatable whether it is served with the flesh of the cock or the hen bird. 1670, Ray.

Best laid schemes gang aft a-gley. The full expression, from Burns's poem 'To a Mouse' (1785), is: The best laid schemes of mice and men gang aft a-gley. *Man's best plans often miscarry.*

I see and approve the better course, but I follow the worse. This is often cited in its Latin form, from Ovid: *Video meliora proboque, deteriora sequor.*
Compare *Romans*, 7, 19: For the good that I would I do not: but the evil which I would not, that I do.

Seeing is believing. 1539, Clarke. Adumbrations of the saying are as old as Aristophanes and Plautus.

Self-preservation is the first law of nature. A. 1614, Donne: It is onely upon this reason that selfe-preservation is of Naturall Law. 1678, Marvell: Self-preservation, nature's first great law.
Yet this would seem to encourage a purely selfish attitude to life—in fact 'Women and children last', not first.

They also serve who only stand and wait. *Even those who cannot work actively can help to serve a good cause.* These words come from the sonnet on his blindness written by Milton, who, after he became blind at the age of forty-four, wrote *Paradise Lost*, *Paradise Regained*, and *Samson Agonistes*. They refer to doing God's will.

Perhaps Milton was thinking of a passage in *Luke*, 10, 42: But one thing is needful: and Mary hath chosen that good part, which shall not be taken away from her.

374

A secret between more than two is no secret. *If more than two know a secret, it will become known by others and will no longer be one.* Another but less common form of the proverb is **Two may keep counsel if one be away.**

A. 1400, *The Romance of the Rose*: For twayne of noumbre is bet than thre In every counsell and secre. 1546, Heywood: We twayne are one to many (quoth I), for men say, Three maie a kepe counsayle, if two be away. The French have *Secret de deux, secret de Dieu; secret de trois, secret de tous* [A secret of two is shared by God; a secret of three is shared by all].

375

Catch not at the shadow and lose the substance. *Do not, by trying to gain something subordinate or trivial, miss reaching what is important.* The allusion is to Aesop's fable where a dog, trying to get a bone that is only a reflection in water of what it has in its mouth, loses even that one. 1579, Lyly: In arguing of the shadowe we forgoe the substance. **R.** 1855, in Bohn's *Handbook of Proverbs*.

376

Out of sight, out of mind. 1275, *Proverbs of Alfred*: He that is ute bi loken he is inne sone forzgeten [He who is shut outside is soon forgotten within]. 1450, Thomas à

Kempis, *De Imitatione Christi* (translation): When man is oute of sight, sone he passith oute of mynde. **R.** 1539, Taverner.

Two other proverbs with the same or similar sense, but now obsolescent or obsolete, are **Long absent, soon forgotten** (which goes back to 1616), and **Far from eye, far from heart** (which goes back to 1300).

On the other hand contrast **Absence makes the heart grow fonder** (1).

377

Silence gives consent. 1380, Wyclif: Oo maner of consent is, whanne a man is stille and tellith not. Chaucer: Lo eke an olde proverbe amonges many other, 'He that is stille semeth as he graunted'. 1490: This proverbe was seide full longe a-go: 'Who so holdeth hym still doth assent'. 1591, Lyly, *Endymion*: Silence, madam, consents. **R.** 1768, Goldsmith's *Good-natur'd Man.*

378

You cannot make a silk purse out of a sow's ear. Figuratively, *It is impossible to turn a person who is by nature coarse or stupid into a refined and cultured person.* **A.** 1514: None can make goodly silke of a gotes fleece. 1611: A man cannot make a cheverill [kid-glove] purse of a sows eare. **R.** 1738, Swift.

379

If you sing before breakfast, you'll cry before night (*or* **dinner**). **A.** 1530: You waxe mery this morning, God gyue grace you wepe nat or nyght. In 1721 Kelly has: They that laugh in the morning may greet e'er night. ('greet' = 'weep' is now obsolete except in Scottish and northern dialects.)

O.D.E.P. gives also **Laugh before breakfast, you'll cry before supper.**

380

There is many a slip between the cup and the lip. *When a person is very near the point of satisfying a desire or gaining an object, something often happens to frustrate him.* The proverb goes back to ancient Greek literature. Mr. Burton Stevenson ascribes its origin to Homer, *Odyssey,* XXII, where Odysseus smites Antinous with an arrow in the throat as he is raising a wine-cup to his lips to drink. Another ascription has been to the story of one Ancaeus, who, told that he would not survive to taste the wine from his grapes, lived until it was ready, and was about to drink some of it when, hearing that a wild boar was laying waste his vineyard, he put down the cup without drinking from it, and rushed out against the boar, by which he was killed.

In Latin literature Cato of Utica (95–46 B.C.) is recorded as having said he had often heard that many things 'could intervene between the mouth and what it was about to bite'; and Horace wrote that 'Many things happen between the cup and the tip of the lip'.

In English literature Taverner, 1539, has: Many things fall between ye cuppe and the mouth. Lyly, 1580, substitutes 'lip' for 'mouth'. **R.** 1824.

381

Slow and (*or* but) sure. A. 1633, Draxe: Slowness is sure. 1639, Fuller (the divine): These, though slow, were sure. **R.** 1692, L'Estrange, in *Æsop's Fables.* 1859, Smiles in *Self-Help* writes 'Provided the dunce has persistency and application he will inevitably head the cleverer fellow without those qualities. Slow but sure wins the race'.

No smoke without fire. Figuratively, *Widespread rumours mean there must be some substance of fact behind them.* A. 1375: And their may no man fire so covir but low or reyk sall it discovir [No-one can cover up fire so that flame and smell will not disclose it].

I am the captain of my soul. *Whatever sufferings I have to endure I will remain in control of my spiritual life.* This is a line from the poem 'Invictus' by W. E. Henley (1849–1903). It expresses a courageous and heroic sentiment that does not reflect the absurd and foolish presumptuousness of the preceding line, 'I am the master of my fate'.

One sows and another reaps. *Work on a thing is done by one person, and the benefit is gained by someone else.* This is an adaptation of *John*, 4, 37: One soweth, and another reapeth.

As you sow, so will you reap. A. eighth century, Cynewulf: Swa eal manna bearn Sorgum sawath swa eft ripath [All the children of men as they sow in sorrow, so afterwards they reap]. *Galatians*, 6, 7: For whatsoever a man soweth, that shall he also reap.

A spaniel, a woman, and a walnut tree, the more they're beaten the better they be. The Romans had a saying: *Nux, asinus, mulier verbere opus habent* [A nut-tree, an ass, and a woman need beating]. 1586, Pettie: I have read, I know not where, these verses, 'A woman, an ass, and a walnut

tree, Bring the more fruite the more beaten they be'.
R. 1670, Ray.

Like many other proverbs, this must have originated
from an extremely cynical mind. We must not take it as an
encouragement, say, of wife-beating.

387

Spare the rod and spoil the child. A. *Proverbs*, 13, 24:
He that spareth his rod hateth his son: but he that loveth
him chastiseth him betimes. 'spoil' is substituted for 'hate'
by Langland, 1377, though he gives it as a translation, from
the Vulgate, of *odit* (Latin), which means 'hates'. R. 1639,
Clarke.

388

Speech is silver, but silence is gold. *Speech produces much
that is delightful and valuable, but there are times when the
most important thing is to say nothing.* The idea is as old as
the Talmud. A. Chaucer: These wyse clerkes that ben
dede Han ever yet proverbed to us yonge, That 'first vertu
is to kepe tonge'. 1470, Ashby: Grete wisdam is, litel to
speke. 1732, Fuller: Silence is wisdom, when speaking is
folly. R. Carlyle, 1831, *Sartor Resartus*: As the Swiss In-
scription says: *Sprechen ist silbern, Schweigen ist golden*
[Speech is silver, Silence is golden].

389

The spirit is willing, but the flesh is weak. *Our higher
nature wishes to do what is right, but our lower desires prevent our doing it.* The words come from *Matthew*, 26, 41.

390

A staff (*or* stick) is quickly found to beat a dog with.
Figuratively, with 'dog' standing for a 'person', *If a person*

has a bad name, it is easy to find ground for complaint against him. 1563, Becon: How easy a thing it is to find a staff if a man be minded to beat a dog. Shakespeare in *II Henry VI* refers to the saying as an 'ancient proverb'.

391

Still waters run deep. Figuratively, *Quiet, undemonstrative, behaviour and manners often have deep emotion underneath.*

There is sometimes in the use of the saying an implication that there is danger from a silent person who never reveals his inner thoughts and intentions.

1400: Ther the flode is deppist the water standis stillist. The earliest record of the figurative use of the expression is in 1858, by Mrs. Craik: In mature age the fullest, tenderest tide of which the loving heart is capable may be described by those 'still waters' which 'run deep'. A deep stream makes no noise; a shallow one, running over stones, makes a loud noise.

392

A stitch in time saves nine. Used both literally and, now more commonly, figuratively. 1732, Fuller: A stitch in time may save nine. **R.** 1869, Charles Reade.

393

Stolen waters (*or* **pleasures) are sweet (***or* **sweetest).** *Proverbs*, 9, 17: Stolen waters are sweet, and bread eaten in secret is pleasant. Compare **Forbidden fruit is sweet** (143).

394

A straw may show which way the wind blows. This expression is generally used metaphorically, meaning that *an extremely slight outward sign may indicate or reveal an inward state of things, or, in a big or important matter, what* *is happening or about to happen, or what a person intends to do.* Bacon's *Essays* (1597): Fling up a straw, 'twill show the way the wind blows. **R.** 1910, E. V. Lucas.

395

Strike while the iron is hot. This metaphor, taken from the smith who shapes the iron while it is hot, is generally used for seizing the right moment, when circumstances are suitable, for making an effort. Chaucer, *Troylus and Cryseyde*: Pandare, which that stood hir faste by, Felte iren hoot, and he bigan to smyte [in making advances to her]. **R.** 1614, Camden.

Compare **Make hay while the sun shines** (174).

396

There is but one step from the sublime to the ridiculous. This is a translation of Napoleon's statement in 1812: *Du sublime au ridicule il n'y a qu'un pas.* 1794, Paine: One step above the sublime makes the ridiculous, suggests that perhaps Napoleon hàd read Paine.

397

Nothing succeeds like success. *The fact that a thing is known to be successful causes it to become even more so.* **R.** 1872 in Besant and Rice's *Ready-money Mortiboy.*

An opposite statement, **Failure is the only highroad to success,** is quoted by Graham Balfour in his *Life of Stevenson* (1902) as 'an old saying'.

398

Sufficient unto (*or* to) the day. This is an abridgement of the statement in *Matthew*, 6, 34, which continues 'is the evil thereof'. *Let the matter rest there, and wait until the* *future discloses itself, without worrying now about what may happen and how to deal with it.*

399

Let not the sun go down upon thy wrath. This injunction is in *Ephesians*, 4, 26, meaning *Do not let anger continue, but put it aside* (strictly, before the day ends and night comes on).

400

Do not swap horses when crossing a stream. Figuratively, *Do not (perhaps with disastrous results) change arrangements while you are in the middle of negotiating a difficulty.* The first record of the use of the expression is in a speech made in 1864 by Abraham Lincoln, who said it had been used to him by an old Dutch farmer. A. Johnson points out in *Common English Proverbs* that travellers used to ride two horses alternately, and, when one was tired, would mount the other.

401

Our sweetest songs are those that tell of saddest thought. This comes from Shelley's ode 'To a Skylark' (1819).

402

Take things as they come. *Accept every event that happens to you with calmness and without complaint or resentment even if it is unpleasant.* 1611, J. Davies's collection of proverbs: Take all things as they come and be content.

403

Talk of the devil, and he is sure to appear. The expression is generally used with reference to a person suddenly and unexpectedly appearing on the scene whose company one would sooner be without. 1666, Torriano, in his book of Italian proverbs, writes 'The English say, Talk of the Devil, and he s presently at your elbow'.

403a

Never spoil a ship for a haporth of tar. The original reference was to losing or spoiling a sheep, ewe, or hog, by stinting the use of tar to protect sores or wounds from flies. 'sheep' is often dialectically pronounced 'ship'. A reference to losing a ship is not recorded before 1861 (by Charles Reade).

404ˑ

Every man (*or* one) to his (*or* one's) taste (*or* own taste). *One must tolerate people's individual likings however strange.* O.D.E.P. and Apperson cite many expressions, with the same meaning, from the sixteenth to the nineteenth century, but all have a different phrase from 'to his (or one's) taste', such as 'to his liking', 'to his mind', 'as he likes', 'as he loveth', until 1759 when Sterne uses 'taste'.

The expression is often supplemented by 'quoth the man (or the woman) when he (or she) kissed his (or her) cow'. This appears in the first record of the proverb, by Heywood in 1546. One wonders whether Heywood invented this jocular adornment.

405

There is no accounting for tastes. The origin of this sentiment is a Latin proverb, *De gustibus non disputandum* [Tastes do not admit of argument]. In English literature **A.** (1) 1599, J. Minsheu: Against one's liking there is no disputing. (2) 1760, Sterne: There is no disputing against hobby-horses. (3) Dr. Johnson, *Lives of the Poets*: Men may be convinced, but they cannot be pleased, against their will. **R.** 1823, Galt.

Give a thief enough rope and he will hang himself. *If he is allowed enough liberty he will end by getting himself hanged.* **A.** 1639, Fuller (the divine), **R.** 1670, Ray.

Second thoughts are best. The idea is expressed in Greek by Euripides, and in Latin by Cicero. In English literature, 1586, Pettie (in his translation from Italian): The second thoughts are euer the best. **R.** 1681, Dryden.
· But Shaftesbury in *Characteristics* (1711) writes: 'Men's first thoughts are generally better than their second', and that sentiment is echoed by Byron and others.

Threatened folk (*or* **folks,** *or* **men) live long.** 1555: It is a true prouerbe: the threatned man lyues long. **R.** 1599.
Compare **A creaking gate hangs long on its hinges (64).**

A tide taken at the flood leads on to fortune. This is from *Julius Caesar* (IV, iii, 217).

Time flies (sometimes expressed in the Latin phrase *Tempus fugit*). Chaucer: For thogh we slepe or wake, or rome or ryde, Ay fleeth the tyme, it nil no man abyde. **R.** 1807, Crabbe. Compare 414.

Time is the great healer and **Time cures all things** are the two forms in which the sentiment is most commonly expressed. *O.D.E.P.* gives **Time (and thinking) tames the strongest grief.** The earliest record of the sentiment is in

[121]

Greek, by Euripides (438 B.C.). Chaucer: As tyme hem hurt, a tyme doth hem cure. 1721, Kelly: Time and thought tame the strongest grief.

411

Time marches on. In a general application, *Time quickly passes*, *Time flies* (see 408); in a particular application, *The time is quickly passing*. Mr. Eric Partridge in his *Dictionary of Clichés* says the expression came into use in the present century.

412

Time is money. *Time is a condition affecting the production of things and the execution of undertakings in which money is made.* 1748, Benjamin Franklin.

413

There is a time to speak and a time to be silent. *Ecclesiastes*, 3, 7: (There is) a time to keep silence, and a time to speak. 1485, Caxton: The comyn prouerbe sayth that there is a tyme of spekyng and tyme of beyng stylle.

414

Time and tide wait (*or* stay, *or* tarry) for no man. Chaucer: For thogh we slepe or wake, or rome, or ryde, Ay fleeth the tyme, it nil no man abyde. 1440: The tid abit [abides] nat for no maner man, Nor stynt his course for no creature. R. 1822, Scott, *The Fortunes of Nigel*, Ch. XXVI. Compare 409.

415

Take time by the forelock. *Act promptly*, or *Seize the present moment*, or *Seize a favourable opportunity*. Time is often represented with a lock of hair on his forehead but none on the rest of his head, signifying that the present time can be used (compare the Latin phrase, *Carpe diem* = 'Seize the day'), but the past cannot be. 1591, Greene: Take time now by the forehead: she is bald behind. Shakespeare, who uses the image in several plays, calls time 'that bald sexton' (*King John*, III, i. 324). **R.** 1883, R. L. Stevenson.

416

Timeo Danaos et dona ferentes. *They are to be feared even though they offer gifts.* *Timeo Danaos* = I fear the Danaans (Greeks). The phrase comes from Virgil's *Aeneid*, II, 48, and is spoken by Laocoon when the Greeks withdrew from the siege of Troy, and pretended to present the Wooden Horse as an offering to Athene.

417

Times change. Of the use of this proverb no printed record appears in the reference books. Mr. Burton Stevenson cites a seventh century phrase, *tempora dum variant* [while times are changing]. In another Latin form an often quoted line is *Tempora mutantur nos et mutamur in illis* [Times change and we with them]. This was attributed to Lothair I, Emperor of the Holy Roman Empire in the ninth century. In the original version the first word, instead of 'Tempora', was 'Omnia' [All things]. The quotation popularised in the sixteenth century appeared first in English literature in Holinshed's *Chronicle* (1577).

418

A bad (*or* ill) workman quarrels with (*or* blames) his tools. 1670, Ray.

419

Every man to his trade (*or* craft, *or* business). Both Greek and Latin (in which the originator was Cicero) have this saying. In English literature **A.** 1539, Taverner: Let euerye man exercise hym selfe in the facultie that he knoeth. **R.** *I Henry IV*, II, ii, 85.

419a

It is better to travel hopefully than to arrive. *More pleasure and interest are gained in the course of journeying in a hopeful spirit to a place one wishes to reach, or aiming hopefully at accomplishing a task or ambition, than in attaining one's aim, which often proves less satisfying than one had expected, and brings disappointment.* The dictum comes from an essay by R. L. Stevenson, 'El Dorado', in *Virginibus Puerisque* (1881): 'To travel hopefully is a better thing than to arrive; the true success is to labour'.

420

Never trouble trouble till trouble troubles you. This is part of a jingling quatrain

> Never trouble trouble
> Till trouble troubles you.
> It only doubles trouble,
> And troubles others too.

A. 1732, Fuller: Let your trouble tarry till its own day comes. The only citations of the quatrain I have found are in 1882 in the *Folk-Lore Journal*, and in 1921 as a West Country saying in a book of essays.
Compare the next article, **Don't meet troubles half way.**

421

Don't meet troubles half way means much the same as the last proverb. **A.** *Much Ado about Nothing*, I, i, 99: You are come to meet your trouble: the fashion of the world is to avoid cost, and you encounter it. **R.** 1896.
Compare **Do not cross the bridge till you come to it** (66).

Many a true word is spoken in jest. Chaucer: Ful ofte in game a soothe [truth] I have herd seye. 1665, *Roxburgh Ballads*: Many a true word hath been spoke in jest. **R.** 1738, Swift.

Truth lies at the bottom of a well. Diogenes Laertius (A.D. 200–250), who wrote in Greek, said 'We know nothing certain, for truth is hidden at the bottom of an abyss'. Later in the same century the Latin writer Lactantius, in a book on Christian doctrine, wrote of truth as 'lying submerged in a well'. Bacon in his *Apophthegms* (1624) described it as 'lying in profound pits and, when it is got, needing much refining'.

Truth is stranger than fiction. *Facts of real life can be stranger than even the most remarkable events and characters one reads about in books.* 1823, Byron, *Don Juan*, For Truth is always strange, stranger than fiction.

Truth will prevail. A. 1390, Gower: Trowthe mot stonde ate laste. 1576, Fulwell: Trueth in the end shall preuayle. The Vulgate has *Magna est veritas, et praevalet* [Great is truth, and it prevails].

Union is strength. Brewer says this proverb is a translation from the Greek of a maxim of Periander, ruler of Corinth (665–555 B.C.), although Homer has the idea in *Iliad* XIII, 237: Union gives strength, even to weak men. I have not been able to find a record of its early use in

English literature. Bacon, 1615, has 'Strength united is the greater'.

426

Verb. sap. An abbreviation of the Latin *Verbum sat sapienti* = (Here is a case where) to a wise man one word is enough. Brewer, instead of 'one word', has 'a hint'. Mr. Burton Stevenson says the phrase was introduced into English by William Dunbar (1465–1530).

427

In vino veritas. (Latin) Literally, *In wine is truth*; figuratively, *Truth comes out of a man when he is drunk*. Mr. Burton Stevenson mentions the beginning of a song, expressing this thought, by the ancient Greek poet Alcaeus, cited in Erasmus's *Adagia* (1550) in Latin.

But contrast **When the wine is in, the wit is out,** i.e. *Wine makes a fool of a man.*

428

Virtue is its own reward. This is a translation of the words of the Latin poet Claudian, who flourished in the early part of the fourth century A.D., and recorded first as used in English literature by Dryden in 1673.

429

The voice of the people is the voice of God. Mr. Burton Stevenson mentions an early expression of this statement by the classical Greek poet Hesiod. In a Latin form, *Vox populi vox Dei*, it appears first in Alcuin (735–804), who denied its truth. From the fourteenth century onwards it is often cited, as true or as false. Pope in *Imitations of Horace* has (Epistle I)

the People's voice is odd.
It is, and it is not, the voice of God.

[126]

Everything comes to him who waits. **A.** 1514: Somewhat shall come who can his time abide. 1642, Torriano, from the Italian: He who can wait hath what he desireth. 1847, Disraeli: Everything comes if a man will only wait. The French have *Tout vient à point à qui sait attendre* [Everything comes in the end to him who knows how to wait].

Walls have ears. This statement is generally used either in an explanation how some secret information etc. became known, or in utterance of a warning to be careful what one says as there may be listeners everywhere. **A.** 1591, Harington, in a translation of *Orlando Furioso*: Posts have eares, and walls have eyes to see. **R.** 1633, Shirley: They say 'Walls have ears'.

It is magnificent, but it is not war. Figuratively, *It is fine, wonderful, admirable, in its way, but it is not what is wanted or suitable for the circumstances, occasion, purpose.* This was originally a translation of an exclamation in French made by Marshal Canrobert in the Crimean War about the Charge of the Light Brigade at Balaklava (1854).

One should not wash one's dirty linen in public. *One should not in public discuss, and make known, private, and especially family, grievances, troubles, quarrels, disputes, scandals.* 1815, Napoleon, *Il faut laver son linge sale en famille*. 1842, Macaulay, quoting Voltaire, See what a quantity of his dirty linen the king sends me to wash. 1867, Trollope, There is nothing I think so bad as washing one's daily linen in public. 1886, E. J. Hardy, *How to be*

Happy Though Married, People should remember the proverb about the washing of soiled linen.

434

Waste not, want not. 1796, Maria Edgeworth. Compare **Wilful waste makes woeful want** (436).

435

A watched pot never boils. 1848, Mrs. Gaskell in *Mary Barton*.

436

Wilful waste makes woeful want. 1721, Kelly. Compare **Waste not, want not** (434).

437

The weakest goes to the wall. 1450: The weykist gothe eyuer [go ever] to the walle. **R.** Shakespeare, *Romeo and Juliet*, I, i, 17.

We may compare this with the doubtful morality of **Self-preservation is the first law of nature** (372).

438

It is better to wear out than to rust out. *When, towards the end of a person's career, he is unable to continue an active life, it is better to reach this stage by having exercised and exhausted his strength and capacities than by having let himself become stagnant.* The allusion is to the contrast between a piece of machinery that, after being well used, is no longer workable, 'is worn out', and one that owing to a state of inactivity is no longer able to be put into operation. **R.** spoken by Bishop Cumberland (1631–1718).

Even the weariest river Winds somewhere safe to sea.
This line from one of Swinburne's most beautiful poems,
'The Garden of Proserpine', is sometimes quoted as
meaning that the worst trouble a man has, and however
long it lasts, eventually comes to an end, and turns to
happiness. The poet, however, is referring to the peaceful
calm of death:

> From too much love of living,
>   From hope and fear set free,
> We thank with brief thanksgiving
>   Whatever gods may be,
> That no man lives for ever,
>   That dead men rise up never,
>   That even the weariest river
>   Winds somewhere safe to sea.

439

All is well that ends well. A. 1300, *Proverbs of Hending*:
Well is him tha wel ende mai. **R.** 1546, Heywood. Then
Shakespeare's *All's Well That Ends Well*.

440

Every why has a (*or* hath its) wherefore. *There is a reason
for everything.* **A.** 1566: I have given you a wherefore for
this why many times. **R.** Shakespeare, *A Comedy of Errors*,
II, ii.

441

Where there's a will there's a way. A. 1640, Herbert: To
him that will, ways are not wanting. In 1836 in Michael
Scott's *Cruise of the Midge* the statement in its current form
is quoted, within inverted commas, as a proverb.

442

He who will not when he may, when he will (*or* would) he shall have nay. There is a tenth-century adumbration of this, of which the translation is: If he now does not want to, while he can, afterwards, when he at last wants to, he will not be able. There are a number of variations in this key from the twelfth to the fourteenth century, and in the sixteenth century a citation in the current form by Heywood. The saying is used now chiefly in the nursery or school-room to mean that, if one does not do a thing when there is an opportunity, later on, when one wants to do it, there will not be one.

443

God tempers the wind to the shorn lamb. ('temper' here = 'regulate', 'restrain', 'check', 'curb'.) The original proverb seems to have been French, where it is found as far back as the end of the sixteenth century, in *Dieu mésure le froid* [the 'cold', instead of the 'wind'] *à la brebis tondue*. 1640, Herbert: To a close shorn lamb God gives wind by measure. Sterne in *A Sentimental Journey* uses the verb 'tempers'.

Today, figuratively, 'temper the wind to the shorn' means 'adopt gentle methods with the weak'.

444

March winds and April showers bring forth May flowers. 1886. Adumbrations and early versions, from the fifteenth to the nineteenth century, refer only to showers in April.

445

Good wine needs no bush. Figuratively, *the merits of a good thing will prove themselves without the need of advertising*. The allusion is to a bunch of ivy, sacred to Bacchus, that was the sign shown outside inns and shops where wine was sold. 1539, Taverner: Wyne that is saleable and good nedeth no bushe or garlands of yvye to be hanged before. Shakespeare in *As You Like It* uses the words figuratively: If it be true that a good wine needs no bush, 'tis true that a good play needs no epilogue.

446

It is easy to be wise after the event. *After an undesirable event has happened it is easy to say what should have been done to prevent it.* A. 1599, Ben Jonson: Away, thou strange justifier of thyself to be wiser than thou wert, by the event! 1875, Jowett (translating Plato): There is no merit in learning wisdom after the event. **R.** Conan Doyle, 1909. Compare **It is easy to prophesy after the event (343).**

447

Don't whistle (*or* halloo, *or* shout) until you are out of the wood. Figuratively, *Don't express premature elation at having escaped a danger, solved a difficulty, etc.* A wood, being a place where one can lose one's way, is taken as a symbol of danger. 1801, Huntington: But alas! I hallooed before I was out of the wood. 1866, Charles Kingsley, *Hereward the Wake,* has 'halloa'. 1897, W. E. Norris has 'shout'. 1922, Mrs. Meynell has 'whistle'.

448

The wish is father to the thought. *We soon believe what we desire.* The thought is expressed in classical Latin literature by Julius Caesar and by Ovid. Chaucer: 'Lo, Lo!' quod dame Prudence, 'how lightly is every man enclynd to his owene desyr and to his owene plesaunce!' *II Henry IV,* IV, v: (PRINCE) 'I never thought to hear you speak again'; (KING HENRY) 'Thy wish was father, Harry, to that thought'.

449

Fair (*or* **Fine**) **words butter no parsnips.** *Flattery and high-sounding promises bring no benefit and are worthless unless accompanied or followed by the action that circumstances call for and one needs.* **R. 1639.**
Compare **Deeds, not words** (79).

450

Hard words break no bones. *Strong, harsh, abusive, language may be unpleasant, but by itself, unless accompanied by action, has no effect.*
In my childhood there was a jingle

> Sticks and stones will break my bones,
> But names will never hurt me.

451

A woman's work is never at an end (never done). A. 1573, T. Tusser: Some respit to husband the weather may send, But huswiues affaires haue neuer an end. The saying must have become proverbial early in the seventeenth century because in 1629 it was the title of a ballad mentioned in the *Stationers' Register.*

451a

Wonders never cease. 1776, in a letter from Sir Henry Dudley to David Garrick

452

Wonders last but nine days. Chaucer, For wonder last but nine days nevere in toune! From Heywood, 1540, to the seventeenth century and later, events were often described as a 'nine day wonder', 'a nine days' wonder at the most', etc., and Shakespeare has 'a day longer than a wonder lasts', 'aware of the nine days out of the wonder', 'these few days' wonder'.

453

Work while it is day. *Concern yourself actively with your earthly task while life is yours.* The injunction comes from *John*, 9, 4: I must work the works of him that sent me, while it is day: the night cometh, when no man can work. It is adapted by Carlyle in *Sartor Resartus* (1836) to 'Work while it is called Today, for the Night cometh wherein no man can work'.

453a

All work and no play makes Jack a dull boy. 1659, Howell.

454

Half (*or* One half of) the world knows not how the other half lives. *O.D.E.P.* gives, as the earliest record of the thought, Rabelais (1532), *La moytié du monde ne sçait comment l'autre vit.* In English literature the first record is by Herbert in 1640.

455

(a) **As well (*or* good) be; (b) Better be, out of the world, (a) as, (b) than out of the fashion.** **R.** 1639, J. Clarke in his collection of English and Latin proverbs. 1738. Swift: Better be out of the world than out of the fashion.

456

It takes all sorts to make a world. **A.** 1620: In the world there must be of all sorts. **R.** D. Jerrold, 1844.

457

Even a worm will turn. *O.D.E.P.* gives a longer form, Tread on a worm and it will turn. Figuratively, *There comes a point when even the meekest and most subservient person will refuse any longer to submit to ill-treatment.* 1546, Heywood: Tread a woorme on the tayle, and it must turne agayne. 'turn' presumably means 'move, not remain quiet and passive'.

458

Two wrongs do not make a right means the same as Two blacks do not make a white (21).

459

Young men see visions; old men dream dreams. This is adapted from *Joel*, 2, 28, quoted by St. Peter in *Acts*, 2, 17. *The young imagine what will or may happen in the future; the thoughts of the old are memories of the past.*

460

If you want a thing well done, do it yourself. A. 1566, Painter: This proverbe olde and true. . . . The thing do not expect by frends to atchieue: which thou thyselfe canst doe, thy selfe for to relieue. 1616, Draxe, *Bibliotheca Scholastica*: If a man will haue his business well done, he must due it himselfe. R. 1858, Longfellow, in *Miles Standish*.

INDEX

The references are to the numbers of the articles (not to pages)

The proverbs are arranged, as far as can be done conveniently, in alphabetical order according to the first or the most significant key word. The List of Proverbs therefore, corresponding to this arrangement, supplies automatically a primary index. The list that now follows is supplementary. To have given here the most significant key word would have been repetitive. Instead, there is given another, and sometimes more than one, secondary key word. This provides a method, alternative to that in the List of Proverbs, for finding the number of a required proverb of which the first or most significant word is now known or remembered.

[136]

[137]

[141]

rosebuds, 150
rough-hew, 87
round, 250
rule, 115
ruat, 133
run, 134, 253, 391
rust, 438

safe, 366, 438a
said, 224
sailor, 357
sand, 236
sap., 426
sauce, 197
save, 324, 392
say, 89, 305
schemes, 369
scorned, 178
sea, 137, 438a
see, 23, 121, 245, 459
seed, 25
seldom, 276
servant, 282
serve, 267, 373
seven, 353
shadow, 55, 375
shapes, 87
sheep, 169, 403a
shepherd, 357
shine, 174, 353
ship, 355, 403a
shorn, 443
short, 5, 78
shortest, 130
shot, 142
shout, 447
show, 394
showers, 444
shut, 219
sick, 191
side, 346
sight, 376
silence, 388
silk, 378

silver, 51, 388
sin, 332
sinews, 283
singly, 276
sinking, 355
skin-deep, 9
skittles, 232
sky, 357
slave, 72
sleeping, 94
slight, 167
slip, 380
slow, 155
slowly, 173
small, 155
smoke, 382
smooth, 253
soft, 4
somewhere, 234, 438a
son, 132
soonest, 224, 300
sorry, 366
sorts, 456
soul, 31, 383
sow, 384, 385
speech, 388
speed, 172
spilt, 67
spoil, 59, 387
spoken, 422
spoon, 83
spots, 227
springs, 192
stable-door, 219
stand, 373
star, 182
statistics, 229
steal, 319
step, 396
stick, 85, 390
stomach, 106
stone, 26, 58, 153, 361
storm, 331
strained, 273

want (v.), 322, 434, 460
war, 127, 164, 283, 322, 432
warning, 357
waste (n.), 436
waste (v.), 139, 434
water, 24, 26, 222, 236, 391, 393
way, 28, 130, 394, 421, 441
weak, 389
weakest, 42, 437
wealthy, 98
wear, 58, 438
weariest, 438a
weeds, 201
weep, 219a
well (adj.), 439
well (adv.), 169, 455, 460
well (n.), 423
west, 185
wherefore, 440
white, 21
whole, 292
why, 440
wife, 194
wilful, 436
will (n.), 441
willing, 389
wind, 202, 394, 443, 444
winds, 438a
window, 333

wine, 427, 445
winter, 165
wise, 98, 199, 446
wit, 31
woeful, 436
woman, 81, 178, 317, 386, 451
won, 126
wonders, 451a, 452
wood, 447
word, 79, 422, 449, 450
work, 103, 167, 449, 451, 452, 453
world, 156, 219a, 250, 292, 451, 453, 453a
worm, 99, 457
worse, 172, 200, 312, 370
worst, 62, 277
worth, 11, 195
worthy, 215
would, 442
wrath, 4, 399
writing, 356
wrong, 209, 458

year, 48, 367
young, 72, 158, 264, 459
yourself, 460
Yule, 165